Mometrix TEST PREPARATION

# MCA

## Success Strategies Grade 7 Mathematics

I0894308

# Dear Future Exam Success Story

First of all, **THANK YOU** for purchasing Mometrix study materials!

Second, congratulations! You are one of the few determined test-takers who are committed to doing whatever it takes to excel on your exam. **You have come to the right place.** We developed these study materials with one goal in mind: to deliver you the information you need in a format that's concise and easy to use.

In addition to optimizing your guide for the content of the test, we've outlined our recommended steps for breaking down the preparation process into small, attainable goals so you can make sure you stay on track.

We've also analyzed the entire test-taking process, identifying the most common pitfalls and showing how you can overcome them and be ready for any curveball the test throws you.

Standardized testing is one of the biggest obstacles on your road to success, which only increases the importance of doing well in the high-pressure, high-stakes environment of test day. Your results on this test could have a significant impact on your future, and this guide provides the information and practical advice to help you achieve your full potential on test day.

**Your success is our success**

**We would love to hear from you!** If you would like to share the story of your exam success or if you have any questions or comments in regard to our products, please contact us at **800-673-8175** or **support@mometrix.com**.

Thanks again for your business and we wish you continued success!

Sincerely,
The Mometrix Test Preparation Team


Written and edited by the Mometrix Test Preparation Team
Printed in the United States of America

# TABLE OF CONTENTS

# Introduction

**Thank you for purchasing this resource**! You have made the choice to prepare yourself for a test that could have a huge impact on your future, and this guide is designed to help you be fully ready for test day. Obviously, it's important to have a solid understanding of the test material, but you also need to be prepared for the unique environment and stressors of the test, so that you can perform to the best of your abilities.

For this purpose, the first section that appears in this guide is the **Success Strategies**. We've devoted countless hours to meticulously researching what works and what doesn't, and we've boiled down our findings to the most impactful steps you can take to improve your performance on the test. We start at the beginning with study planning and move through the preparation process, all the way to the testing strategies that will help you get the most out of what you know when you're finally sitting in front of the test.

We recommend that you start preparing for your test as far in advance as possible. However, if you've bought this guide as a last-minute study resource and only have a few days before your test, we recommend that you skip over the first two Success Strategies since they address a long-term study plan.

If you struggle with **test anxiety**, we strongly encourage you to check out our recommendations for how you can overcome it. Test anxiety is a formidable foe, but it can be beaten, and we want to make sure you have the tools you need to defeat it.

# Strategy #1 – Plan Big, Study Small

There's a lot riding on your performance. If you want to ace this test, you're going to need to keep your skills sharp and the material fresh in your mind. You need a plan that lets you review everything you need to know while still fitting in your schedule. We'll break this strategy down into three categories.

## Information Organization

Start with the information you already have: the official test outline. From this, you can make a complete list of all the concepts you need to cover before the test. Organize these concepts into groups that can be studied together, and create a list of any related vocabulary you need to learn so you can brush up on any difficult terms. You'll want to keep this vocabulary list handy once you actually start studying since you may need to add to it along the way.

## Time Management

Once you have your set of study concepts, decide how to spread them out over the time you have left before the test. Break your study plan into small, clear goals so you have a manageable task for each day and know exactly what you're doing. Then just focus on one small step at a time. When you manage your time this way, you don't need to spend hours at a time studying. Studying a small block of content for a short period each day helps you retain information better and avoid stressing over how much you have left to do. You can relax knowing that you have a plan to cover everything in time. In order for this strategy to be effective though, you have to start studying early and stick to your schedule. Avoid the exhaustion and futility that comes from last-minute cramming!

## Study Environment

The environment you study in has a big impact on your learning. Studying in a coffee shop, while probably more enjoyable, is not likely to be as fruitful as studying in a quiet room. It's important to keep distractions to a minimum. You're only planning to study for a short block of time, so make the most of it. Don't pause to check your phone or get up to find a snack. It's also important to **avoid multitasking**. Research has consistently shown that multitasking will make your studying dramatically less effective. Your study area should also be comfortable and well-lit so you don't have the distraction of straining your eyes or sitting on an uncomfortable chair.

The time of day you study is also important. You want to be rested and alert. Don't wait until just before bedtime. Study when you'll be most likely to comprehend and remember. Even better, if you know what time of day your test will be, set that time aside for study. That way your brain will be used to working on that subject at that specific time and you'll have a better chance of recalling information.

Finally, it can be helpful to team up with others who are studying for the same test. Your actual studying should be done in as isolated an environment as possible, but the work of organizing the information and setting up the study plan can be divided up. In between study sessions, you can discuss with your teammates the concepts that you're all studying and quiz each other on the details. Just be sure that your teammates are as serious about the test as you are. If you find that your study time is being replaced with social time, you might need to find a new team.

# Strategy #2 – Make Your Studying Count

You're devoting a lot of time and effort to preparing for this test, so you want to be absolutely certain it will pay off. This means doing more than just reading the content and hoping you can remember it on test day. It's important to make every minute of study count. There are two main areas you can focus on to make your studying count.

## Retention

It doesn't matter how much time you study if you can't remember the material. You need to make sure you are retaining the concepts. To check your retention of the information you're learning, try recalling it at later times with minimal prompting. Try carrying around flashcards and glance at one or two from time to time or ask a friend who's also studying for the test to quiz you.

To enhance your retention, look for ways to put the information into practice so that you can apply it rather than simply recalling it. If you're using the information in practical ways, it will be much easier to remember. Similarly, it helps to solidify a concept in your mind if you're not only reading it to yourself but also explaining it to someone else. Ask a friend to let you teach them about a concept you're a little shaky on (or speak aloud to an imaginary audience if necessary). As you try to summarize, define, give examples, and answer your friend's questions, you'll understand the concepts better and they will stay with you longer. Finally, step back for a big picture view and ask yourself how each piece of information fits with the whole subject. When you link the different concepts together and see them working together as a whole, it's easier to remember the individual components.

Finally, practice showing your work on any multi-step problems, even if you're just studying. Writing out each step you take to solve a problem will help solidify the process in your mind, and you'll be more likely to remember it during the test.

## Modality

*Modality* simply refers to the means or method by which you study. Choosing a study modality that fits your own individual learning style is crucial. No two people learn best in exactly the same way, so it's important to know your strengths and use them to your advantage.

For example, if you learn best by visualization, focus on visualizing a concept in your mind and draw an image or a diagram. Try color-coding your notes, illustrating them, or creating symbols that will trigger your mind to recall a learned concept. If you learn best by hearing or discussing information, find a study partner who learns the same way or read aloud to yourself. Think about how to put the information in your own words. Imagine that you are giving a lecture on the topic and record yourself so you can listen to it later.

For any learning style, flashcards can be helpful. Organize the information so you can take advantage of spare moments to review. Underline key words or phrases. Use different colors for different categories. Mnemonic devices (such as creating a short list in which every item starts with the same letter) can also help with retention. Find what works best for you and use it to store the information in your mind most effectively and easily.

# Strategy #3 – Practice the Right Way

Your success on test day depends not only on how many hours you put into preparing, but also on whether you prepared the right way. It's good to check along the way to see if your studying is paying off. One of the most effective ways to do this is by taking practice tests to evaluate your progress. Practice tests are useful because they show exactly where you need to improve. Every time you take a practice test, pay special attention to these three groups of questions:

- The questions you got wrong
- The questions you had to guess on, even if you guessed right
- The questions you found difficult or slow to work through

This will show you exactly what your weak areas are, and where you need to devote more study time. Ask yourself why each of these questions gave you trouble. Was it because you didn't understand the material? Was it because you didn't remember the vocabulary? Do you need more repetitions on this type of question to build speed and confidence? Dig into those questions and figure out how you can strengthen your weak areas as you go back to review the material.

Additionally, many practice tests have a section explaining the answer choices. It can be tempting to read the explanation and think that you now have a good understanding of the concept. However, an explanation likely only covers part of the question's broader context. Even if the explanation makes perfect sense, **go back and investigate** every concept related to the question until you're positive you have a thorough understanding.

As you go along, keep in mind that the practice test is just that: practice. Memorizing these questions and answers will not be very helpful on the actual test because it is unlikely to have any of the same exact questions. If you only know the right answers to the sample questions, you won't be prepared for the real thing. **Study the concepts** until you understand them fully, and then you'll be able to answer any question that shows up on the test.

It's important to wait on the practice tests until you're ready. If you take a test on your first day of study, you may be overwhelmed by the amount of material covered and how much you need to learn. Work up to it gradually.

On test day, you'll need to be prepared for answering questions, managing your time, and using the test-taking strategies you've learned. It's a lot to balance, like a mental marathon that will have a big impact on your future. Like training for a marathon, you'll need to start slowly and work your way up. When test day arrives, you'll be ready.

Start with the strategies you've read in the first two Success Strategies—plan your course and study in the way that works best for you. If you have time, consider using multiple study resources to get different approaches to the same concepts. It can be helpful to see difficult concepts from more than one angle. Then find a good source for practice tests. Many times, the test website will suggest potential study resources or provide sample tests.

## Practice Test Strategy

If you're able to find at least three practice tests, we recommend this strategy:

### Untimed and Open-Book Practice

Take the first test with no time constraints and with your notes and study guide handy. Take your time and focus on applying the strategies you've learned.

### Timed and Open-Book Practice

Take the second practice test open-book as well, but set a timer and practice pacing yourself to finish in time.

### Timed and Closed-Book Practice

Take any other practice tests as if it were test day. Set a timer and put away your study materials. Sit at a table or desk in a quiet room, imagine yourself at the testing center, and answer questions as quickly and accurately as possible.

Keep repeating timed and closed-book tests on a regular basis until you run out of practice tests or it's time for the actual test. Your mind will be ready for the schedule and stress of test day, and you'll be able to focus on recalling the material you've learned.

# Strategy #4 – Pace Yourself

Once you're fully prepared for the material on the test, your biggest challenge on test day will be managing your time. Just knowing that the clock is ticking can make you panic even if you have plenty of time left. Work on pacing yourself so you can build confidence against the time constraints of the exam. Pacing is a difficult skill to master, especially in a high-pressure environment, so **practice is vital**.

Set time expectations for your pace based on how much time is available. For example, if a section has 60 questions and the time limit is 30 minutes, you know you have to average 30 seconds or less per question in order to answer them all. Although 30 seconds is the hard limit, set 25 seconds per question as your goal, so you reserve extra time to spend on harder questions. When you budget extra time for the harder questions, you no longer have any reason to stress when those questions take longer to answer.

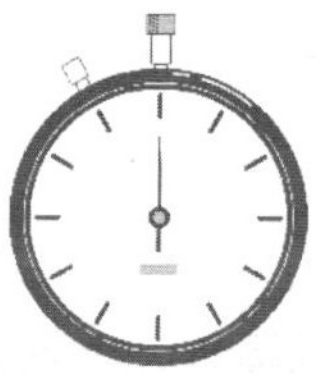

Don't let this time expectation distract you from working through the test at a calm, steady pace, but keep it in mind so you don't spend too much time on any one question. Recognize that taking extra time on one question you don't understand may keep you from answering two that you do understand later in the test. If your time limit for a question is up and you're still not sure of the answer, mark it and move on, and come back to it later if the time and the test format allow. If the testing format doesn't allow you to return to earlier questions, just make an educated guess; then put it out of your mind and move on.

On the easier questions, be careful not to rush. It may seem wise to hurry through them so you have more time for the challenging ones, but it's not worth missing one if you know the concept and just didn't take the time to read the question fully. Work efficiently but make sure you understand the question and have looked at all of the answer choices, since more than one may seem right at first.

Even if you're paying attention to the time, you may find yourself a little behind at some point. You should speed up to get back on track, but do so wisely. Don't panic; just take a few seconds less on each question until you're caught up. Don't guess without thinking, but do look through the answer choices and eliminate any you know are wrong. If you can get down to two choices, it is often worthwhile to guess from those. Once you've chosen an answer, move on and don't dwell on any that you skipped or had to hurry through. If a question was taking too long, chances are it was one of the harder ones, so you weren't as likely to get it right anyway.

On the other hand, if you find yourself getting ahead of schedule, it may be beneficial to slow down a little. The more quickly you work, the more likely you are to make a careless mistake that will affect your score. You've budgeted time for each question, so don't be afraid to spend that time. Practice an efficient but careful pace to get the most out of the time you have.

# Test-Taking Strategies

This section contains a list of test-taking strategies that you may find helpful as you work through the test. By taking what you know and applying logical thought, you can maximize your chances of answering any question correctly!

It is very important to realize that every question is different and every person is different: no single strategy will work on every question, and no single strategy will work for every person. That's why we've included all of them here, so you can try them out and determine which ones work best for different types of questions and which ones work best for you.

## Question Strategies

### ✓ Read Carefully

Read the question and the answer choices carefully. Don't miss the question because you misread the terms. You have plenty of time to read each question thoroughly and make sure you understand what is being asked. Yet a happy medium must be attained, so don't waste too much time. You must read carefully and efficiently.

### ✓ Contextual Clues

Look for contextual clues. If the question includes a word you are not familiar with, look at the immediate context for some indication of what the word might mean. Contextual clues can often give you all the information you need to decipher the meaning of an unfamiliar word. Even if you can't determine the meaning, you may be able to narrow down the possibilities enough to make a solid guess at the answer to the question.

### ✓ Prefixes

If you're having trouble with a word in the question or answer choices, try dissecting it. Take advantage of every clue that the word might include. Prefixes can be a huge help. Usually, they allow you to determine a basic meaning. *Pre-* means before, *post-* means after, *pro-* is positive, *de-* is negative. From prefixes, you can get an idea of the general meaning of the word and try to put it into context.

### ✓ Hedge Words

Watch out for critical hedge words, such as *likely, may, can, often, almost, mostly, usually, generally, rarely*, and *sometimes*. Question writers insert these hedge phrases to cover every possibility. Often an answer choice will be wrong simply because it leaves no room for exception. Be on guard for answer choices that have definitive words such as *exactly* and *always*.

### ✓ Switchback Words

Stay alert for *switchbacks*. These are the words and phrases frequently used to alert you to shifts in thought. The most common switchback words are *but, although*, and *however*. Others include *nevertheless, on the other hand, even though, while, in spite of, despite*, and *regardless of*. Switchback words are important to catch because they can change the direction of the question or an answer choice.

### ☑ Face Value

When in doubt, use common sense. Accept the situation in the problem at face value. Don't read too much into it. These problems will not require you to make wild assumptions. If you have to go beyond creativity and warp time or space in order to have an answer choice fit the question, then you should move on and consider the other answer choices. These are normal problems rooted in reality. The applicable relationship or explanation may not be readily apparent, but it is there for you to figure out. Use your common sense to interpret anything that isn't clear.

## Answer Choice Strategies

### ☑ Answer Selection

The most thorough way to pick an answer choice is to identify and eliminate wrong answers until only one is left, then confirm it is the correct answer. Sometimes an answer choice may immediately seem right, but be careful. The test writers will usually put more than one reasonable answer choice on each question, so take a second to read all of them and make sure that the other choices are not equally obvious. As long as you have time left, it is better to read every answer choice than to pick the first one that looks right without checking the others.

### ☑ Answer Choice Families

An answer choice family consists of two (in rare cases, three) answer choices that are very similar in construction and cannot all be true at the same time. If you see two answer choices that are direct opposites or parallels, one of them is usually the correct answer. For instance, if one answer choice says that quantity *x* increases and another either says that quantity *x* decreases (opposite) or says that quantity *y* increases (parallel), then those answer choices would fall into the same family. An answer choice that doesn't match the construction of the answer choice family is more likely to be incorrect. Most questions will not have answer choice families, but when they do appear, you should be prepared to recognize them.

### ☑ Eliminate Answers

Eliminate answer choices as soon as you realize they are wrong, but make sure you consider all possibilities. If you are eliminating answer choices and realize that the last one you are left with is also wrong, don't panic. Start over and consider each choice again. There may be something you missed the first time that you will realize on the second pass.

### ☑ Avoid Fact Traps

Don't be distracted by an answer choice that is factually true but doesn't answer the question. You are looking for the choice that answers the question. Stay focused on what the question is asking for so you don't accidentally pick an answer that is true but incorrect. Always go back to the question and make sure the answer choice you've selected actually answers the question and is not merely a true statement.

### ☑ Extreme Statements

In general, you should avoid answers that put forth extreme actions as standard practice or proclaim controversial ideas as established fact. An answer choice that states the "process should be used in certain situations, if..." is much more likely to be correct than one that states the "process should be discontinued completely." The first is a calm rational statement and doesn't even make a definitive, uncompromising stance, using a hedge word *if* to provide wiggle room, whereas the second choice is far more extreme.

### ⊘ Benchmark

As you read through the answer choices and you come across one that seems to answer the question well, mentally select that answer choice. This is not your final answer, but it's the one that will help you evaluate the other answer choices. The one that you selected is your benchmark or standard for judging each of the other answer choices. Every other answer choice must be compared to your benchmark. That choice is correct until proven otherwise by another answer choice beating it. If you find a better answer, then that one becomes your new benchmark. Once you've decided that no other choice answers the question as well as your benchmark, you have your final answer.

### ⊘ Predict the Answer

Before you even start looking at the answer choices, it is often best to try to predict the answer. When you come up with the answer on your own, it is easier to avoid distractions and traps because you will know exactly what to look for. The right answer choice is unlikely to be word-for-word what you came up with, but it should be a close match. Even if you are confident that you have the right answer, you should still take the time to read each option before moving on.

## General Strategies

### ⊘ Tough Questions

If you are stumped on a problem or it appears too hard or too difficult, don't waste time. Move on! Remember though, if you can quickly check for obviously incorrect answer choices, your chances of guessing correctly are greatly improved. Before you completely give up, at least try to knock out a couple of possible answers. Eliminate what you can and then guess at the remaining answer choices before moving on.

### ⊘ Check Your Work

Since you will probably not know every term listed and the answer to every question, it is important that you get credit for the ones that you do know. Don't miss any questions through careless mistakes. If at all possible, try to take a second to look back over your answer selection and make sure you've selected the correct answer choice and haven't made a costly careless mistake (such as marking an answer choice that you didn't mean to mark). This quick double check should more than pay for itself in caught mistakes for the time it costs.

### ⊘ Pace Yourself

It's easy to be overwhelmed when you're looking at a page full of questions; your mind is confused and full of random thoughts, and the clock is ticking down faster than you would like. Calm down and maintain the pace that you have set for yourself. Especially as you get down to the last few minutes of the test, don't let the small numbers on the clock make you panic. As long as you are on track by monitoring your pace, you are guaranteed to have time for each question.

### ⊘ Don't Rush

It is very easy to make errors when you are in a hurry. Maintaining a fast pace in answering questions is pointless if it makes you miss questions that you would have gotten right otherwise. Test writers like to include distracting information and wrong answers that seem right. Taking a little extra time to avoid careless mistakes can make all the difference in your test score. Find a pace that allows you to be confident in the answers that you select.

### ✓ KEEP MOVING

Panicking will not help you pass the test, so do your best to stay calm and keep moving. Taking deep breaths and going through the answer elimination steps you practiced can help to break through a stress barrier and keep your pace.

## Final Notes

The combination of a solid foundation of content knowledge and the confidence that comes from practicing your plan for applying that knowledge is the key to maximizing your performance on test day. As your foundation of content knowledge is built up and strengthened, you'll find that the strategies included in this chapter become more and more effective in helping you quickly sift through the distractions and traps of the test to isolate the correct answer.

Now that you're preparing to move forward into the test content chapters of this book, be sure to keep your goal in mind. As you read, think about how you will be able to apply this information on the test. If you've already seen sample questions for the test and you have an idea of the question format and style, try to come up with questions of your own that you can answer based on what you're reading. This will give you valuable practice applying your knowledge in the same ways you can expect to on test day.

**Good luck and good studying!**

# Mathematics

## Ratio and Proportion

A ratio is a comparison of two numbers by division. The ratio of $a$ to $b$, where $b \neq 0$, can be written as

$$a \text{ to } b$$
$$a{:}\,b$$
$$\frac{a}{b}$$

A proportion is a statement of equality between two ratios. For example, $\frac{a}{b} = \frac{c}{d}$, where $b \neq 0$ and $d \neq 0$, is a proportion equating the ratios $\frac{a}{b}$ and $\frac{c}{d}$.

## Integer

The set of integers includes whole numbers and their opposites: {...,-3,-2,-1,0,1,2,3...}.

## Rational Number

A rational number is a real number which can be written as a ratio of two integers $a$ and $b$, where $b \neq 0$ so long as the second is not zero; in other words, any rational number can be expressed in fractional form $\frac{a}{b}$, where $b \neq 0$. Rational numbers include whole numbers, fractions, terminating, and repeating decimals.

### *Example*

Write each rational number as a fraction

- 3
- 0.6

Since dividing any number by one does not change its value, a whole number can be written as a fraction with a denominator of 1. So, $3 = \frac{3}{1}$.

The six in 0.6 is in the tenths place. The number six-tenths can also be written as $\frac{6}{10}$, which reduces to $\frac{3}{5}$.

### *EXAMPLE*

Simply each expression

$$\frac{2}{3}+\frac{1}{2}$$

$$\frac{2}{3}-\frac{1}{2}$$

When combining fractions, it is helpful to write them so that they have the same denominator.

**1.**

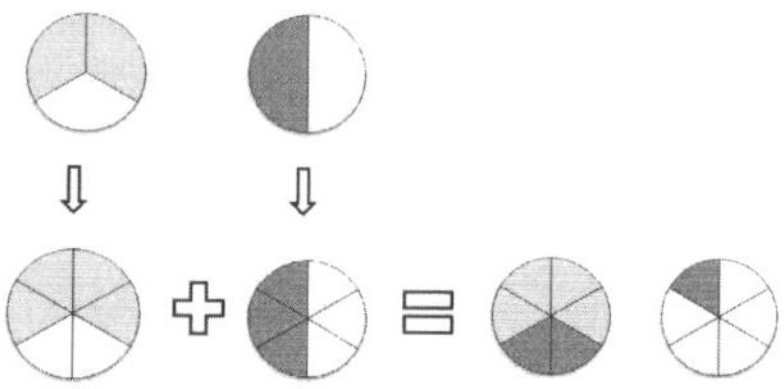

$$\frac{2}{3}=\frac{4}{6} \qquad \frac{1}{2}=\frac{3}{6}$$

$$\frac{4}{6}+\frac{3}{6}=\frac{7}{6}=1\frac{1}{6}$$

2.

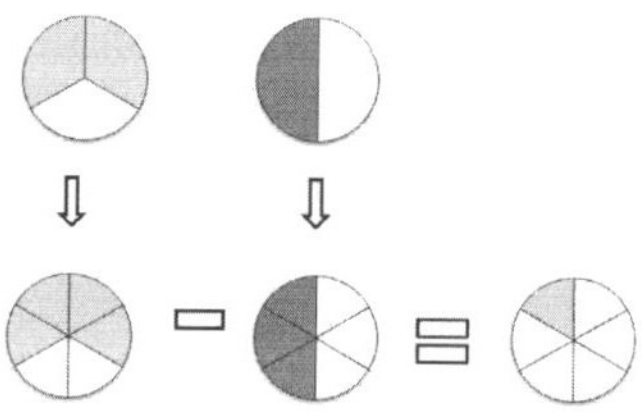

$$\frac{4}{6}-\frac{3}{6}=\frac{1}{6}$$

### *EXAMPLE*

Simplify each expression

$$\frac{1}{2}\times\frac{2}{3}$$

$$\frac{1}{8}\div\frac{1}{2}$$

The numerator of the product of two fractions is the product of their numerators; $1 \times 2 = 2$. Likewise, the denominator of the product of two fractions is the product of their denominators: $2 \times 3 = 6$. Reduce the resulting fraction if necessary.

$$\frac{1}{2}\times\frac{2}{3}=\frac{2}{6}=\frac{1}{3}$$

When dividing fractions, rewrite the expression as the product of the first fraction and the reciprocal (or multiplicative inverse) of the second. Reduce if necessary.

$\frac{1}{8}\div\frac{1}{2}=\frac{1}{8}\times\frac{2}{1}=\frac{2}{8}=\frac{1}{4}$;

### *EXAMPLE*

Convert each fraction to a decimal.

$$\frac{4}{5}$$
$$\frac{5}{6}$$

A fraction is a quotient of two numbers such that the denominator is not zero. So, one way to convert a fraction to a decimal is to divide the denominator into the numerator. The resulting decimal will either terminate or repeat.

$$\frac{4}{5} = 4 \div 5 = 0.8$$

```
   0.8
5 |4.0
   0 ↓
   4 0
   4 0
     0
```

$$\frac{5}{6} = 5 \div 6 = 0.8\overline{3}$$

```
   0.833...
6 |5.000...
   0 ↓
   5 0
   4 8↓
     20
     18↓
      20
      18
       2
```

## PERCENTAGE

One *Percent* means one part per hundred, so a percentage is the ratio of a number to 100. For example, 42% can be written as the ratio $\frac{42}{100}$ or its reduced equivalent, $\frac{21}{50}$.

### *EXAMPLE*

Write each percentage as a simplified fraction and as a decimal

- 32%
- 135%

A percentage is a ratio of a number to 100.

$$32\% = \frac{32}{100} = \frac{8}{25} \; or \; \frac{32}{100} = 0.32$$

$$135\% = \frac{135}{100} = 1\frac{35}{100} = 1\frac{7}{20}$$

$$\frac{135}{100} = 1\frac{35}{100} = 1.35$$

### *Example*

Write each number as a percentage

$$\frac{4}{5}$$

$$\frac{2}{3}$$

$$0.23 = \frac{23}{100} = 23\%$$

$$\frac{4}{5} = \frac{80}{100} = 80\%$$

$$\frac{2}{3} = 0.\bar{6} = 66.\bar{6}\%$$

### *Example*

Express the shaded portion of the circle as a fraction, a decimal, and a percentage.

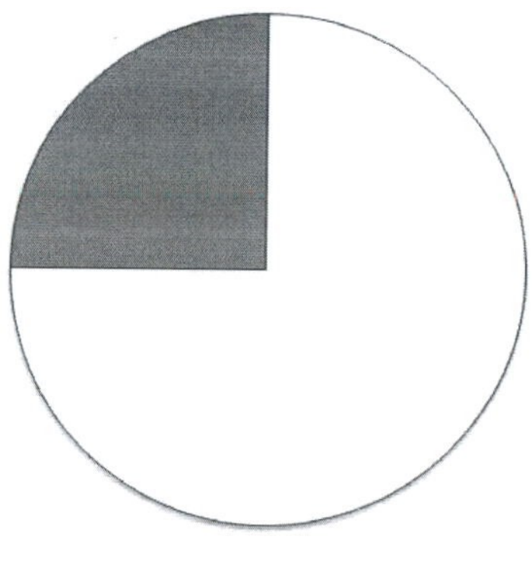

¼ of the circle's area is shaded. $\frac{1}{4} = 0.25 = \frac{25}{100} = 25\%$.

## Determining Whether or Not Two Ratios Form a Proportion

Two ratios form a proportion if they are equal. One way to determine if two ratios are equal is to write each ratio as a fraction (as long as neither contains a zero in its denominator) and then cross-multiply: that is, multiply the numerator of the first fraction and the denominator of the second; then, multiply the denominator of the first fraction and the numerator of the second. If these two products are equal, the ratios are equal and therefore form a proportion. $\frac{a}{b} = \frac{c}{d}$ if and only if $a \times d = b \times c$. For example, $\frac{2}{3} = \frac{12}{18}$, and $2 \times 18 = 3 \times 12 = 36$.

## UNIT RATE

A unit rate is a ratio of two different types of numbers, the second of which is always one. For example, a unit rate can be the number of miles driven in one hour (miles per hour), the price for one ounce of cereal (cents per ounce), or an hourly wage (dollars per hour).

### *EXAMPLE*

A girl walks half a mile in fifteen minutes. Calculate the unit rate in miles per hour

Since there are sixty minutes in an hour, fifteen minutes is a quarter of an hour: $\frac{15}{60} = \frac{1}{4}$. Since the girl walks ½ mile in ¼ hour, her rate can be written as $\frac{\frac{1}{2}\text{ mile}}{\frac{1}{4}\text{ hour}}$. To determine the unit rate, simplify the fraction so that the denominator is one hour. One way to divide by the fraction $\frac{1}{4}$ is to instead multiply by its reciprocal $\frac{4}{1}$. We get $\frac{1}{2} \div \frac{1}{4} = \frac{1}{2} \times \frac{4}{1} = \frac{4}{2} = 2$. The unit rate is two miles per hour.

### *EXAMPLE*

A one pound box of cereal costs \$3.20. Calculate the unit price in dollars per ounce

There are sixteen ounces in a pound, so ratio of the price of cereal to its weight can be written as $\frac{\$3.20}{16\text{ oz}}$. To determine the unit price, find the equivalent ratio which compares the price of the cereal to one ounce. To simplify the ratio, divide both the numerator and denominator by 16. Since $\frac{3.20 \div 16}{16 \div 16} = \frac{0.20}{1}$, the unit price of the cereal is twenty cents per ounce.

### *EXAMPLE*

A bag of 20 cough drops costs \$1.68, and a bag of 50 cough drops costs \$4.20. Determine which is a better deal

To determine which is the better deal, first find the unit prices of the products. For a bag of 20 cough drops at \$1.68, the unit price is $\frac{\$1.68}{20\text{ cough drops}} = \frac{\$0.084}{1\text{ cough drop}}$, or 8.4 cents per cough drop. For a bag of 50 cough drops at \$4.20, the unit price is $\frac{\$4.20}{50\text{ cough drops}} = \frac{\$0.084}{1\text{ cough drop}}$, or 8.4 cents per cough drop. Neither bag is a better bargain than the other since both cost the same amount per cough drop.

### *EXAMPLE*

Determine what it means for two quantities to have a proportional relationship.

When two quantities have a proportional relationship, there exists a **constant of proportionality** between the quantities. The product of this constant and one of the quantities is equal to the other quantity. For example, if one lemon costs \$0.25, two lemons cost \$0.50, and three lemons cost \$0.75, there is a proportional relationship between the total cost of lemons and the number of lemons purchased. The constant of proportionality is the unit price, namely \$0.25/lemon. Notice that the total price of lemons, $t$, can be found by multiplying the unit price of lemons, $p$, and the number of lemons, $n$: $t = pn$.

## Determining Whether Two Quantities Have a Proportional Relationship in a Graph

If two quantities are graphed on the coordinate plane, and the result is a straight line through the origin, then the two quantities are proportional.

### Example

For the graphs below, determine whether there exists a proportional relationship between $x$ and $y$. If a proportional relationship exists, find the constant of proportionality and write an equation for the line.

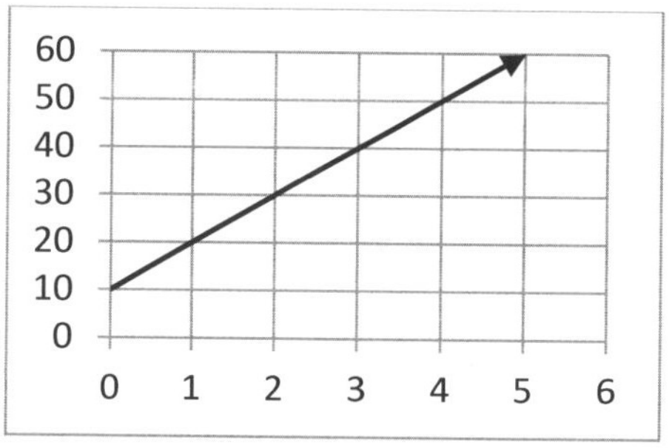


Though the graph of the relationship between x and y is a straight line, it does not pass through the origin. So, though $y$ varies directly as $x$, the ratio $\frac{y}{x}$ is not constant: for instance, $\frac{20}{1} \neq \frac{30}{2} \neq \frac{40}{3}$..

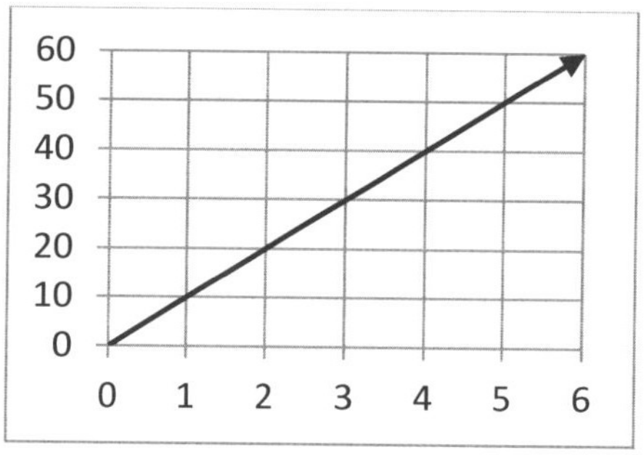


The graph of a proportional relationship is a straight line through the origin.

This graph is a straight line through the origin, so the relationship between $x$ and $y$ is proportional. The constant of proportionality is represented by the ratio $\frac{y}{x}$. This constant is the same as the unit rate. The constant of proportionality is equal to the $y$-value when $x = 1$. Since the ratio $\frac{y}{x}$ is 10 (see that $\frac{y}{x} = \frac{10}{1} = \frac{20}{2} = \frac{30}{3}$ and so on), or since $y = 10$ when $x = 1$, the constant of proportionality is 10. The relationship between $x$ and $y$ is represented by the equation $y = 10x$.

## Determining Whether Two Quantities Have a Proportional Relationship Given a Table of Values

If the ratio of $y$ to $x$ is constant for all values of $x$ and $y$ besides zero, then there is a proportional relationship between the two variables. The value $\frac{y}{x}$ is the constant of proportionality.

### Example

Determine whether there exists a proportional relationship between $x$ and $y$. If a proportional relationship exists, find the constant of proportionality and write an equation to represent the relationship.

If the ratio of $y$ to $x$ is constant for all values of $x$ and $y$ besides zero, then there is a proportional relationship between the two variables. The value $\frac{y}{x}$ is the constant of proportionality.

| x | 1 | 2 | 3 | 4 |
|---|---|---|---|---|
| y | 5 | 9 | 13 | 17 |

The ratio of $y$ to $x$ is not constant; therefore, the values in the table do not represent a proportional relationship:

| x | 1 | 2 | 3 | 4 |
|---|---|---|---|---|
| y | 5 | 9 | 13 | 17 |
| $\frac{y}{x}$ | $\frac{5}{1} = 5$ | $\frac{9}{2} = 4.5$ | $\frac{13}{3} = 4.\overline{3}$ | $\frac{17}{4} = 4.25$ |

### *Example*

Determine whether there exists a proportional relationship between $x$ and $y$. If a proportional relationship exists, find the constant of proportionality and write an equation to represent the relationship.

| x | 1 | 2 | 3 | 4 |
|---|---|---|---|---|
| y | 1 | 4 | 9 | 16 |

If the ratio of $y$ to $x$ is constant for all values of $x$ and $y$ besides zero, then there is a proportional relationship between the two variables. The value $\frac{y}{x}$ is the constant of proportionality.

The ratio of $y$ to $x$ is not constant; therefore, the values in the table do not represent a proportional relationship:

| x | 1 | 2 | 3 | 4 |
|---|---|---|---|---|
| y | 1 | 4 | 9 | 16 |
| $\frac{y}{x}$ | $\frac{1}{1} = 1$ | $\frac{4}{2} = 2$ | $\frac{9}{3} = 3$ | $\frac{16}{4} = 4$ |

### *Example*

Determine whether there exists a proportional relationship between $x$ and $y$. If a proportional relationship exists, find the constant of proportionality and write an equation to represent the relationship.

| x | 1 | 2 | 3 | 4 |
|---|---|---|---|---|
| y | 2.5 | 5 | 7.5 | 10 |

If the ratio of $y$ to $x$ is constant for all values of $x$ and $y$ besides zero, then there is a proportional relationship between the two variables. The value $\frac{y}{x}$ is the constant of proportionality.

The ratio of $y$ to $x$ is 2.5; therefore, the values in the table represent the proportional relationship modeled by the equation $y = 2.5x$:

| x | 1 | 2 | 3 | 4 |
|---|---|---|---|---|
| y | 2.5 | 5 | 7.5 | 10 |
| $\frac{y}{x}$ | $\frac{2.5}{1} = 2.5$ | $\frac{5}{2} = 2.5$ | $\frac{7.5}{3} = 2.5$ | $\frac{10}{4} = 2.5$ |

### Example

Suppose gasoline costs $3 per gallon. Create a table of values for the total cost of gasoline and the gallons of gasoline purchased.

The graph is confined to the first-quadrant of the coordinate plane because neither the amount of gas nor the price of the gas can be negative. Since the cost depends on the number of gallons purchased, plot the number of gallons along the horizontal axis and the cost along the vertical axis.

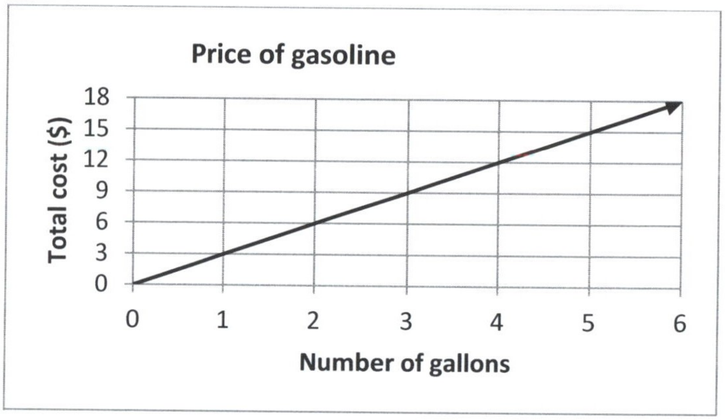


### Example

Create a graph of the relationship between the total cost and the gallons of gasoline purchased

The graph is confined to the first-quadrant of the coordinate plane because neither the amount of gas nor the price of the gas can be negative. Since the cost depends on the number of gallons purchased, plot the number of gallons along the horizontal axis and the cost along the vertical axis.

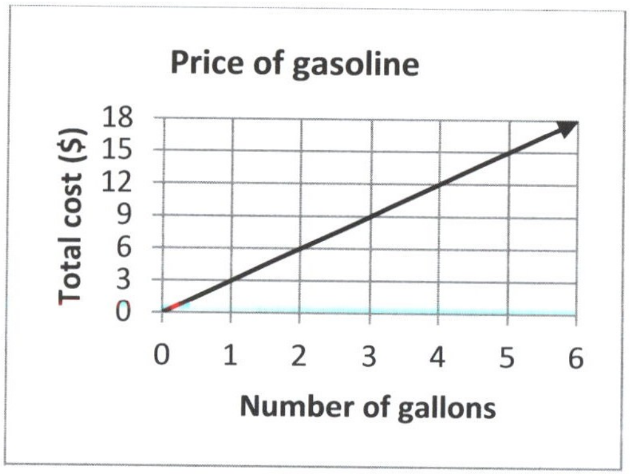


Write an equation which relates total cost to gallons of gasoline purchased.

The equation for the line is y=3x, or total cost=3×number of gallons purchased.

### *Example*

Find the rate of travel from a graph representing a proportional relationship between travel time in hours (graphed along the horizontal axis) and distance traveled in miles (graphed along the vertical axis).

The slope of the line represents the rate of travel, or the proportionality constant, in miles per hour. The slope of a line is its vertical change, or rise, divided by its horizontal change, or run. These values can be determined from by counting the vertical and horizontal distances between any two points on the line or by using the equation $\frac{y_2-y_1}{x_2-x_1}$, where $(x_1, y_1)$ and $(x_2, y_2)$ are points on the line.

A point on the line shows the distance traveled at a particular travel time. Since the ratio of distance to time is constant along the graph representing a proportion relationship, any point on the graph can be used to find the rate by simply finding the ratio of $y$ to $x$. For example, a point (3,90) on the graph indicates that it takes three hours to travel ninety miles, so the rate is $\frac{90\ miles}{3\ hours}$= 30 miles per hour.

Since the unit rate, miles per hour, compares the distance traveled in miles to one hour, the unit rate is the y-coordinate when x=1. For example, if the line passes through (1,30), the rate is 30 miles per hour.

## Using Proportions to Solve Percent Problems

A proportion is a statement of equivalence between two ratios. In percent problems, both ratios compare parts to a whole; in particular, a percentage expresses parts per 100. A proportion which can be used to solved a percent problem is $\frac{part}{whole} = \frac{percent}{100}$.

In the given scenario, 4 is 80% of some number $a$, so 4 represents part of the unknown number. The proportion, therefore, is $\frac{4}{a} = \frac{80}{100}$. There are many ways to solve proportions. Notice that $\frac{80}{100}$ reduces to $\frac{4}{5}$, so $a = 5$.

### *Example*

A family of six dines at a restaurant which charges an automatic gratuity for parties of six or more. A tip of $28 is added to their bill of $80. Determine the percent gratuity charged.

One way to determine the percent gratuity charged is to set up and solve a proportion of the form

$$\frac{part}{whole} = \frac{percent}{100}.$$

$$\frac{28}{80} = \frac{p}{100}$$

There are many ways to solve proportions. Notice that $\frac{28}{80}$ reduces to $\frac{7}{20}$, which can easily be converted to a fraction with a denominator of 100 by multiplying the numerator and denominator by 5.

$$\frac{7 \times 5}{20 \times 5} = \frac{35}{100}$$

So, $p = 35$. The gratuity added is 35%.

### EXAMPLE

The ratio of flour to sugar in a cookie recipe is 3:1. Find the amount of sugar needed for 1 ½ cups of flour

There are many ways to solve this problem using proportional reasoning. One way is to notice that the amount of flour divided by three gives the amount of sugar.

cups of flour: cups of sugar

$$\overset{\div 3}{3:1}$$

So, the amount of sugar needed for 1 ½ cups of flour can be found by dividing $1\frac{1}{2}$ by 3. $1\frac{1}{2} \div 3 = \frac{3}{2} \times \frac{1}{3} = \frac{3}{6} = \frac{1}{2}$.

$$\overset{\div 3}{1\frac{1}{2} : \frac{1}{2}}$$

The amount of sugar needed is ½ cup.

### EXAMPLE

Suppose you purchase a $7.00 entrée and a $2.00 drink at your favorite restaurant.

- Determine the amount of a 10% tax on your purchase.
- Determine the amount of a 15% tip on the pre-tax amount.
- Find the total price of the meal, including tax and tip.

The amount of your purchase before tax and tip is $9.00. There are many way to calculate the amount of tax on the purchase. One method is to set up and solve a proportion:

The amount of the tax will be calculated as a fraction of the purchase price. That fraction comparing the tax amount to the pre-tax price is equal to 10%, or $\frac{10}{100}$. So, $\frac{\textit{tax amount}}{\$9.00} = \frac{10}{100}$. A tax amount of $0.90 satisfies the proportion.

Another method involves translating the problem into a mathematical expression which represents the tax amount, which is *10% of the purchase*.

A percent is a ratio out of 100, so $10\% = \frac{10}{100} = 0.10$.

The word "of" indicates multiplication.

The purchase price is \$9.

So, *10% of the purchase* translates to $0.10 \times \$9$, which equals \$0.90.

Again, there are many ways to calculate the amount of the tip. 15% of \$9.00 translates to $0.15 \times \$9$, which equals \$1.35.

The total price is the cost of the meal plus the tax plus the tip: $\$9.00 + \$0.90 + \$1.35 = \$11.25$.

### Example

A number is decreased by 20%. The resulting number is then increased by 20%. Determine whether the consequent number is greater than, less than, or equal to the original number

If a number is decreased by 20%, and the resulting number is increased by 20%, then the consequent number will be less than the original number.

Consider, for instance, that the original number is 100.

20% of 100 is $0.20 \times 100 = 20$, and $100 - 20 = 80$.

20% of 80 is $0.20 \times 80 = 16$, and $80 + 16 = 96$.

96 is less than 100.

### Example

A school has 400 students; 220 of these students are girls. If the ratio of boys to girls in a class of twenty is representative of the ratio of boys to girls school-wide, determine how many boys are in the class.

Since the ratio of boys to girls in the class is equal to the ratio of boys to girls in the school, the ratio of boys to students in the class must also equal to the ratio of boys to students in the school.

$$\frac{\text{Number of boys in the school}}{\text{number of students in the school}} = \frac{\text{number of boys in the class}}{\text{number of students in the class}}$$

In a school of 400 students, 220 of which are girls, there are $400 - 220 = 180$ boys. The ratio of boys to total students is 180/400, which reduces to 9/20. So, in the class of twenty students, there must be nine boys.

Check to see that the ratio of boys to girls in the class is indeed equal to ratio school-wide. If there are nine boys in a class of twenty, then there are eleven girls:

$$\frac{9 \text{ boys}}{11 \text{ girls}} = \frac{180 \text{ boys}}{220 \text{ girls}}$$

One way to determine whether or not this statement is true is to cross multiply. If the products are equal, then so are the ratios.

$$9 \times 220 = 1980$$

$$11 \times 180 = 1980$$

### *EXAMPLE*

Use a number line to find the sum of 2.1 and 3.2.

Plot 2.1 on a number line and move three and two tenths spaces to the right.

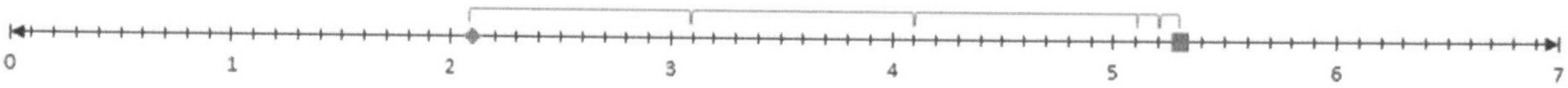


## ADDITIVE INVERSE

The sum of a number and its additive inverse, or opposite, is the additive identity, 0.

### *EXAMPLE*

Find the additive inverse of

3
-5
$x$

The additive inverse of 3 is -3 because $3 + (-3) = 0$.

The additive inverse of -5 is 5 because $-5 + 5 = 0$.

The additive inverse of $x$ is $-x$because $x + (-x) = 0$.

## MULTIPLICATIVE INVERSE

The product of a number and its multiplicative inverse is the multiplicative identity, 1. The multiplicative inverse of a number is also called its reciprocal. The reciprocal of a non-zero rational number is also rational. Zero does not have a multiplicative because the product of zero and any number is zero and can therefore not equal 1 and because zero can never be in the denominator of a fraction.

### *EXAMPLE*

Find the multiplicative inverse of

$$5$$

$$-\frac{2}{3}$$

$x$ such that $x \neq 0$.

The multiplicative inverse of 5 is $\frac{1}{5}$ because $5\left(\frac{1}{5}\right) = 1$.

The multiplicative inverse of $-\frac{2}{3}$ is $-\frac{3}{2}$ because $-\frac{2}{3}\left(-\frac{3}{2}\right) = 1$.

The multiplicative inverse of $x$ is $\frac{1}{x}$ when $x \neq 0$ because $x\left(\frac{1}{x}\right) = 1$when $x \neq 0$.

### EXAMPLE

An atom of oxygen has eight positively charged protons and eight negatively charged electrons

- Determine the charge of an atom of oxygen.
- When an atom gains or loses electrons, it becomes an ion. Determine the charge of an oxygen ion which contains two more electrons than an oxygen atom.

An atom of oxygen has a charge of zero because it has the same number of positively charged protons as it does negatively charged electrons: $8 + (-8) = 0$.

An oxygen ion has a charge of -2 because the neutral atom has gained two negatively charged electrons: $0 + (-2) = -2$ or $8 + (-10) = -2$.

### EXAMPLE

Using number lines, show that 2 ½ − 2 ½ = 2 ½ + (−2 ½) = −2 ½ + 2 ½ = 0.

To subtract 2 ½ from 2 ½ on a number line, start at 2 ½ and move two and a half spaces to the left.

2 ½ − 2 ½ = 0

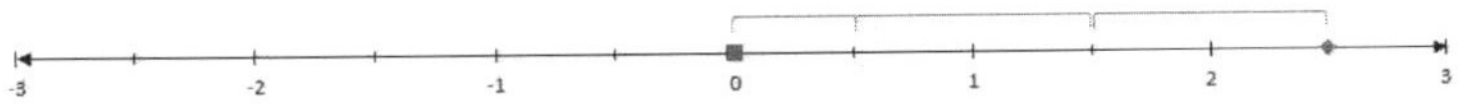


To simplify 2 ½ + (−2 ½) on a number line, start at 2 ½ and move two and a half spaces to the left. 2 ½ + (−2 ½) = 0.

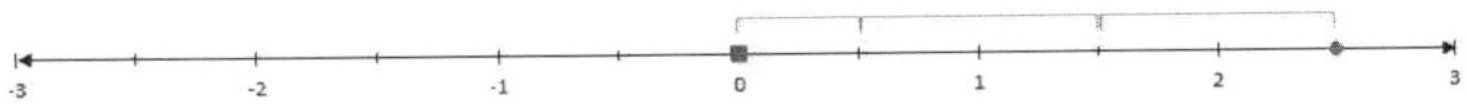


Notice that adding -2 ½ to 2 ½ is that same subtracting 2 ½ from 2 ½.

To add 2 ½ to -2 ½ on a number line, start at -2 ½ and move two and a half spaces to the right. −2 ½ + 2 ½ = 0

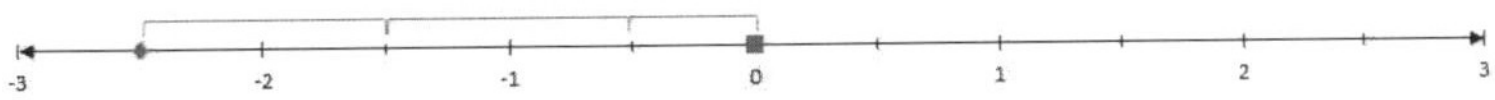


As always, the sum of a number and its opposite is zero.

2 ½ − 2 ½ = 2 ½ + (−2 ½) = −2 ½ + 2 ½ = 0

Example

Express each as a positive or negative number. Then, write a phrase to represent the number's opposite.

- A gain of four yards
- A deduction of ten points

- A 5°F drop in temperature
- A debit of $1.60
- An extra half-mile

A gain of four yards → $+\mathbf{4}$ yards. The opposite is *a loss of four yards*, or $-\mathbf{4}$ yards.

A deduction of ten points → $-\mathbf{10}$ points. The opposite is *an addition of 10 points*, or $+\mathbf{10}$ points.

A 5°F drop in temperature → $-\mathbf{5}$°F. The opposite is *an increase in temperature of 5 °F*, or $+\mathbf{5}$°F.

A debit of $1.60→ $-\$\mathbf{1.60}$. The opposite is *a credit of $1.60*, or $+\$\mathbf{1.60}$.

An extra half-mile→ +½ mile. The opposite is *a half-mile less*, or −½ mile

## Absolute Value

The absolute value of a number is the number's distance from zero on a number line. A measure of distance is always positive, so absolute value is always positive.

### *Example*

Show that $|3|=|-3|$.

The absolute value of 3, written as $|3|$, is 3 because the distance between 0 and 3 on a number line is three units. Likewise, the absolute value of -3, written as $|-3|$, is 3 because the distance between 0 and -3 on a number line is three units. So, $|3|=|-3|$.

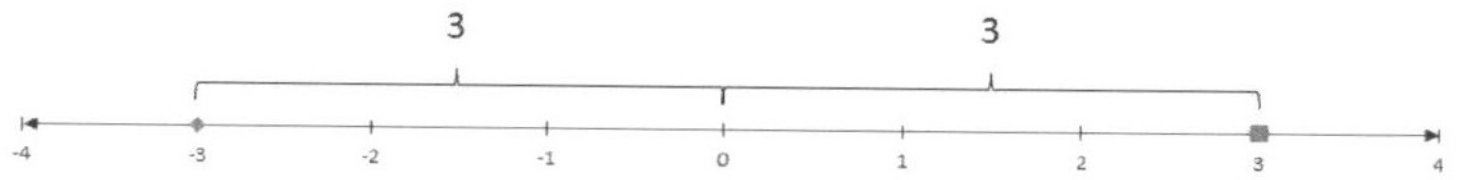


## Multiplying and Dividing Positive and Negative Numbers

The product or quotient of two positive numbers is positive.

$$2 \times 4 = 8$$

$$18 \div 3 = 6$$

The product or quotient of two negative numbers is positive.

$$(-3)(-1) = 3$$

$$\frac{-18}{-9} = 2$$

The product or quotient of a positive and a negative number or a negative and a positive number is negative.

$$4(-2) = -8$$
$$-3 \times 6 = -18$$
$$\frac{20}{-10} = -2$$
$$-15 \div 3 = -5$$

### EXAMPLE

For integers $p$ and $q$, $q \neq 0$, $-\left(\frac{p}{q}\right) = \frac{-p}{q} = \frac{p}{-q}$. Illustrate this property using an example.

Choose an integer value for p and a non-zero integer value for q to show that $-\left(\frac{p}{q}\right) = \frac{-p}{q} = \frac{p}{-q}$. For instance, when p=10 and q=2,

$$-\left(\frac{p}{q}\right) = -\left(\frac{10}{2}\right) = -5$$
$$\frac{-p}{q} = \frac{-10}{2} = -5$$
$$\frac{p}{-q} = \frac{10}{-2} = -$$

### EXAMPLE

A jacket is marked 75% off. Determine which of these methods will give the discounted price of the jacket.

- Find 75% of the jacket's original price and subtract the result from the original price.
- Find 25% of the jacket's original price.
- Divide the original price by four.

All of these methods will give the discounted price of the jacket. If x is the jacket's original price, its new price is $x - 0.75x$. This expression simplifies to $0.25x$. $0.25 = \frac{25}{100} = \frac{1}{4}$, so 0.25x can be rewritten as $\frac{1}{4}x$, which equals $\frac{x}{4}$.

### EXAMPLE

A person plans to lose ½ pound each week by following a healthy diet. Write and simplify an expression to show his expected weight loss after six weeks of healthy eating

A loss of ½ pound each week for six weeks translates to $\left(-\frac{1}{2}\right)(6)$, which simplifies to -3. He can expect to lose three pounds in six weeks.

### EXAMPLE

A gymnast's routine has a start value of 16 points. During her routine, she incurs three deductions of one-tenth of a point, two deductions of three-tenths of a point, and one deduction of half a point. Determine the score she receives for her performance.

Write an expression to represent the gymnast's score. Each deduction is subtracted from her start value. Write all the deductions as fractions or as decimals. $\frac{1}{10} = 0.1$; $\frac{3}{10} = 0.3$; $\frac{1}{2} = 0.5$.

$$16 - 3(0.1) - 2(0.3) - 0.5$$
$$16 - 0.3 - 0.6 - 0.5$$
$$15.7 - 0.6 - 0.5$$
$$15.1 - 0.5 = 14.6$$

The gymnast's score is 14.6.

### EXAMPLE

A service provider charges \$25.75 for phone, \$27.75 for internet, and \$33.50 for cable each month. A one-time credit of \$35.50 is applied towards a customer's bill when the customer opts to prepay for service by quarterly bank draft. After a new customer orders phone, internet, and cable service and signs up for automatic bill pay, she notices a transaction on her bank statement of -\$225.50. Write an expression which justifies this charge made by the service provider.

If the customer pays her bill quarterly, then she pays for three months of service at one time. So, her bill includes three times the total for the phone charge and the internet charge and the cable charge. A credit of \$35.00 is given only once.

$$\begin{aligned}&3[(-\$25.75) + (-\$27.75) + (-\$33.50)] + \$35.00\\&= 3(-\$87.00) + \$35.50\\&= -\$261.00 + \$35.50\\&= -\$225.50\end{aligned}$$

## COMMUTATIVE PROPERTY OF ADDITION AND MULTIPLICATION

The commutative property of addition states that the order in which two numbers are added does not change their sum; the commutative property of multiplication states that the order in which two numbers are multiplied does not change their product.

$$a + b = b + a$$

$$ab = ba$$

## ASSOCIATIVE PROPERTY OF ADDITION AND MULTIPLICATION

The associate property of addition states that a series of added numbers can be grouped in various ways without affecting the sum; the associative property of multiplication states that a series of multiplied numbers can be grouped in various ways without affecting the product.

$$a + (b + c) = (a + b) + c$$

$$a(bc) = (ab)c$$

## ADDITIVE IDENTITY AND THE MULTIPLICATIVE IDENTITY

The additive identity is the number which can be added to a number without changing its value; that number is zero. The multiplicative identity is the number which can be multiplied by a number without changing its value; that number is one.

### EXAMPLE

Use the distributive property to simplify $-\frac{1}{2}(x - 8)$.

The distributive property states that $a(b + c) = ab + ac$ and $a(b - c) = ab - ac$.

$$-\frac{1}{2}(x - 8) = \left(-\frac{1}{2}\right)(x) - \left(-\frac{1}{2}\right)(8) = -\frac{1}{2}x + 4.$$

### *EXAMPLE*

Name the property used in each step of simplifying $\frac{3}{4} \cdot \frac{2}{3} + \frac{3}{4} \cdot \frac{1}{3}$.

$$\frac{3}{4} \cdot \frac{2}{3} + \frac{3}{4} \cdot \frac{1}{3} = \frac{3}{4}\left(\frac{2}{3} + \frac{1}{3}\right)$$
$$\frac{3}{4}\left(\frac{2}{3} + \frac{1}{3}\right) = \frac{3}{4}(1)$$
$$\frac{3}{4}(1) = \frac{3}{4}$$

| | |
|---|---|
| $\frac{3}{4} \cdot \frac{2}{3} + \frac{3}{4} \cdot \frac{1}{3} = \frac{3}{4}\left(\frac{2}{3} + \frac{1}{3}\right)$ | Distributive property |
| $\frac{3}{4}\left(\frac{2}{3} + \frac{1}{3}\right) = \frac{3}{4}(1)$ | Substitution property of equality<br>(Since $\frac{2}{3} + \frac{1}{3} = 1$, the number 1 can replace the expression $\frac{2}{3} + \frac{1}{3}$.) |
| $\frac{3}{4}(1) = \frac{3}{4}$ | Multiplicative identity |

### *EXAMPLE*

Simplify.

$$-\frac{2}{3}\left(a - \frac{1}{4}\right)$$
$$\left(\frac{3}{4}x + 4\right) + \left(\frac{1}{4}x - 3\right)$$

Use the distributive property to simplify $-\frac{2}{3}\left(a - \frac{1}{4}\right)$.

$$\begin{aligned} -\frac{2}{3}\left(a - \frac{1}{4}\right) &= -\frac{2}{3} \cdot a + \left(-\frac{2}{3}\right)\left(-\frac{1}{4}\right) \\ &= -\frac{2}{3}a + \frac{2}{12} \\ &= -\frac{2}{3}a + \frac{1}{6} \end{aligned}$$

Use the associative and commutative properties of addition to simplify $\left(\frac{3}{4}x + 4\right) + \left(\frac{1}{4}x - 3\right)$.

$$\begin{aligned} \left(\frac{3}{4}x + 4\right) + \left(\frac{1}{4}x - 3\right) &= \frac{3}{4}x + 4 + \frac{1}{4}x - 3 \\ &= \frac{3}{4}x + \frac{1}{4}x + 4 - 3 \\ &= x + 1 \end{aligned}$$

### Example

Factor $\frac{1}{2}$ from the expression $\frac{1}{4}x - \frac{1}{2}$.

To factor $\frac{1}{2}$ from the expression $\frac{1}{4}x - \frac{1}{2}$, divide each term in the expression by $\frac{1}{2}$.

$$\frac{1}{4}x \div \frac{1}{2} = \frac{1}{4} \cdot x \cdot \frac{2}{1} = \frac{1}{4} \cdot \frac{2}{1} \cdot x = \frac{2}{4} \cdot x = \frac{1}{2}x$$
$$-\frac{1}{2} \div \frac{1}{2} = -1$$

The factored expression is $\frac{1}{2}\left(\frac{1}{2}x - 1\right)$.

## Words and/or Phrases

### Addition

Some words and phrases that indicate addition are sum, plus, total, and, increased by, more, together, added to, combined with, gain.

### Subtraction

Some words and phrases that indicate subtraction are difference, minus, less, decreased by, take away, fewer than, from, subtracted from, loss.

### Multiplication

Some words and phrases that indicate multiplication are product, times, multiplied by, of, twice/double (×2), thrice/triple (×3).

### Division

Some words and phrases that indication division are quotient, divided by, into, among, between, over, per, for every, ratio of, out of.

These lists are not exhaustive.

### Example

Joshua calculates that the product of $19\frac{3}{4}$ and $10\frac{1}{4}$ is $404\frac{7}{8}$. Use mental estimation to determine the reasonableness of his answer.

The product of two numbers is found by multiplying those numbers, so the product of $19\frac{3}{4}$ and $10\frac{1}{4}$ is about 200 since $19\frac{3}{4}$ is close to 20 and $10\frac{1}{4}$ is close to 10. An answer of $404\frac{7}{8}$ seems unreasonable, so Joshua should check his calculation.

### Example

Suppose you wish to center a 3 ¼ ft wide painting over a buffet which is 5 ¾ ft wide. Approximate how far each edge of the painting would be from each edge of the buffet.

The painting is just over 3 ft wide, and the buffet is just under 6 feet wide. So, the difference in the width of the buffet and the painting is about 3 ft.. The painting is centered above the buffet, half of the difference in width will be space to the left of the painting and the other half will be space to the right of the painting. Half of 3 ft is

1 ½ ft. So, each edge of the painting should be about 1 ½ ft from each edge of the buffet.

## Mathematical Symbols

= equals, is equal to, is, was, were, will be, yields, is the same as, amounts to, becomes

>**is** greater than, **is** more than

≥ **is** greater than or equal to, is at least, is no less than

<**is** less than, **is** fewer than

≤ **is** less than or equal to, is at most, is no more than

### Example

Write three sentences which would translate into the inequality $2(x + 4) \geq 6$.

There are many ways to write $2(x + 4) \geq 6$ as a sentence, including

Two times the sum of a number and four is greater than or equal to six.

Twice the quantity $x$ increased by four is at least six.

The product of two and a number to which four has been added must be no less than six.

### Example

An \$80 dress is marked down 25%. Find the price of the dress after the discount.

One way to find the price of the dress after the discount is to calculate the amount of the discount and subtract it from the price of the dress:

The amount of the discount is 25% of \$80, or $0.25 \times \$80 = \$20$.

The price of the dress after the discount is $\$80 - \$20 = \$60$.

Another way to find the discounted price is to write, simplify, and evaluate an expression representing the problem:

- If $p$ = original price, then $0.25p$ represents the amount of the discount. So, an expression for the new price of the dress is $p - 0.25p$, which simplifies to $0.75p$. In other words, the discounted price of the dress is 75% of the original price. $0.75p = 0.75(\$80) = \$60$.

### Example

If $px$ represents the price of an item, write an expression can be used to find

- The price of the item with 8% sales tax.
- The pre-tax price of the item during a half-off sale.
- The after-tax price of the item during a half-off sale.

The amount of an 8% sales tax added to an item which costs $p$x dollars is $0.08p$. The price of the item with the sales tax is $p + 0.08p$, which simplifies to $\mathbf{1.08p}$.

If the item is half off, the amount of the discount is $\frac{1}{2}p$ . The new price of the item is the original price minus the discount, or $-\frac{1}{2}p$ , which simplifies to $\frac{1}{2}\boldsymbol{p}$.

The price of the half-off item with 8% sales tax is $1.08\left(\frac{1}{2}p\right) = 1.08(0.5p) = \mathbf{0.54}\boldsymbol{p}$.

## DETERMINING THE ORDER OF OPERATIONS USED TO SIMPLIFY EXPRESSIONS

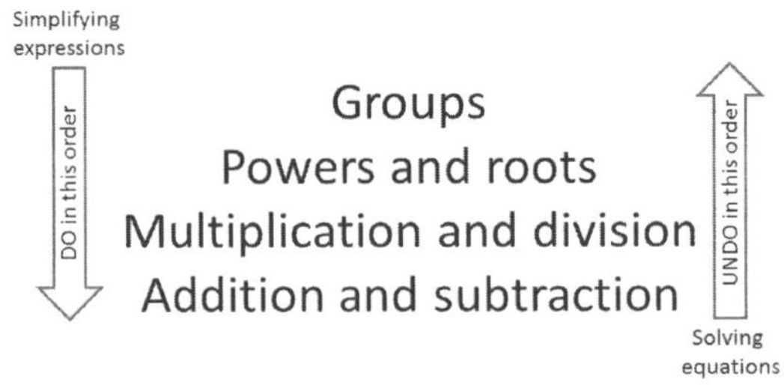


When simplifying an expression, work first within groups, which can be found within grouping symbols such as parentheses but also can be found under radical signs, in numerators or denominators of fractions, as exponents, etc. without such grouping symbols. Next, simplify powers and roots. Then multiply and divide from left to right; finally, add and subtract from left to right.

### *RELATE THIS TO THE SEQUENCE OF OPERATIONS USED WHEN SOLVING EQUATIONS*

When solving an equation, it is often helpful to first use order of operations to simplify the expressions on both sides of the equation, if possible. Then, undo the operations which have been performed on the variable by using inverse operations in reverse order of operations.

### *EXAMPLE*

Alina spent \$20 at the fair. She paid \$2 for admission plus \$1.50 for every ride. Write and solve an equation to determine how many rides she rode.

Let $x =$ the number of rides Alina rode at the fair. The expression $\$1.50x$ represents the amount of money spent riding rides. Alina spent a total of $\$1.50x + \$2$ on rides and admission; this amount equals \$20, so

$$\begin{aligned} \$1.50x + \$2 &= \$20 \\ -\$2 \quad &\;\; -\$2 \\ \hline \$1.50x + \$0 &= \$18 \\ \frac{\$1.50x}{\$1.50} &= \frac{\$18}{\$1.50} \\ x &= 12 \end{aligned}$$

Alina rode twelve rides at the fair.

### *EXAMPLE*

24 feet of fencing was used to enclose a rectangular garden with a width of 8 feet. Write and solve an equation to determine the length of the garden.

The perimeter of a rectangle can be found using the expression $2l + 2w$, where $l$ is the rectangle's length and $w$ is its width. The perimeter of the garden is 24 feet, and the width of the garden is 8 feet, so

$$\begin{aligned} 2l + 2(8) &= 24 \\ 2l + 16 &= 24 \\ -16 \quad &-16 \\ \hline 2l + 0 &= 8 \\ \frac{2l}{2} &= \frac{8}{2} \\ l &= 4 \end{aligned}$$

The length of the garden is 4 feet.

### Example

Leng receives a weekly allowance of five dollars when he completes his usual chores. He can earn an additional fifty cents for each additional chore he does. Write and solve an inequality to find the number of extra chores he should do to earn at least ten dollars this week.

Let $n =$ the number of extra chores Leng must complete. For every extra chore, he earns \$0.50, so $0.5n$ represents the amount of money, in dollars, he will earn from the extra chores. The total amount of money he earns in dollars is represented by the expressions $0.5n + 5$. This weeks, he wishes to earn at least \$10, so he wants to either earn \$10 or more than \$10. Thus, the inequality $5 + 0.5n \geq 10$ represents this scenario.

$$\begin{aligned} 0.5n + 5 &\geq 10 \\ -5 \quad &-5 \\ 0.5n + 0 &\geq 5 \\ \frac{0.5}{0.5}n &\geq \frac{5}{0.5} \\ n &\geq 10 \end{aligned}$$

Leng must complete at least 10 extra chores to earn \$10 or more.

### Example

On a map, the distance between two cities measures 2 ½ inches. A distance of one inch on the map represents an actual distance of 30 miles. Find the actual distance between the two cities.

Use proportional reasoning to find the distance between the two cities. One way to set up a proportion from the given information is to equate two ratios which compare inches to miles, where x represents the unknown distance between the two cities in miles.

$$\frac{2\frac{1}{2}}{x} = \frac{1}{30}$$

There are many ways to solve a proportion. One way is to cross-multiply.

$$\begin{aligned} 2\frac{1}{2} \times 30 &= x \times 1 \\ \frac{5}{2} \times \frac{30}{1} &= x \end{aligned}$$

$$\frac{150}{2} = x$$
$$75 = x$$

The distance between the cities is 75 miles.

### *Example*

A room has dimensions of 12' wide by 15' long. Using a scale of 1/4":1', draw a blueprint of the room.

First, determine the dimensions of the room on the blueprint. Let $w$ represent the width in inches and $l$ represent the length in inches of the room on the scale drawing.

$$\frac{\frac{1}{4}\text{ in}}{1\text{ ft}} = \frac{w}{12\text{ ft}}$$

Using cross-multiplication, $1 \cdot w = \left(\frac{1}{4}\right)(12) = 3$. The width of the room on the blueprint is 3 in.

$$\frac{\frac{1}{4}\text{ in}}{1\text{ ft}} = \frac{l}{15\text{ ft}}$$

Again using cross-multiplication, $1 \cdot l = \left(\frac{1}{4}\right)(15) = \frac{15}{4} = 3\frac{3}{4}$. The length of the room on the blueprint is $3\frac{3}{4}$in.

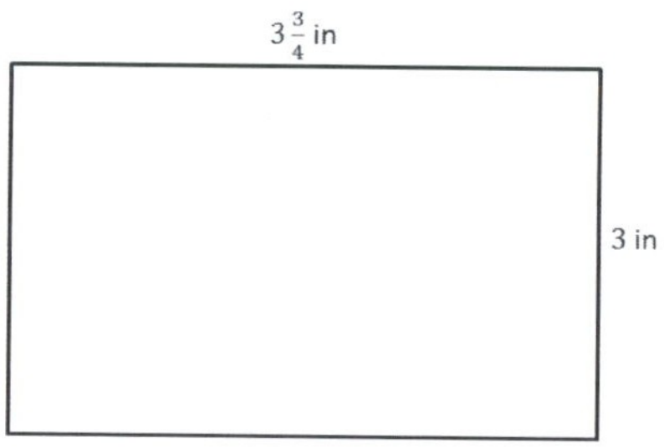


### *Example*

Below is a box drawn at 1:4 scale.

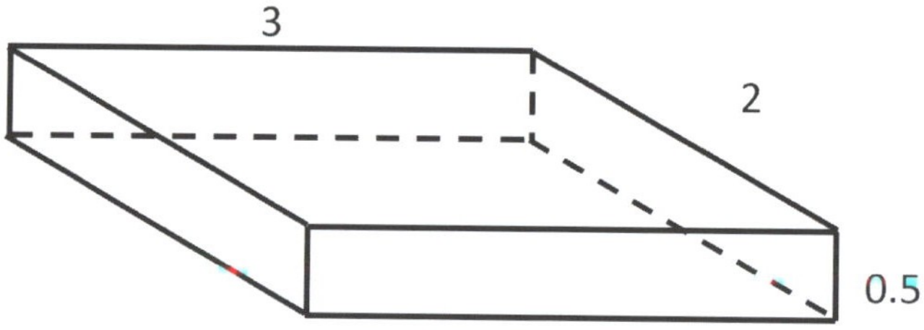


Draw the box at a scale of 1:8.

Determine the actual dimensions of the box.

A scale of 1:4 mean that each side of the box is $\frac{1}{4}$ the size of the actual box.

Redrawing at a scale of 1:8 means that each side of the drawing will be $\frac{1}{8}$ the size of the actual box, or $\frac{1}{2}$ of the size of the given scale drawing since $\frac{1}{2} \times \frac{1}{4} = \frac{1}{8}$. So, draw a box whose dimensions are half of the length, width, and height of the given scale drawing. Since ½=0.5, use either number to calculate the new dimensions.
$0.5 \times 3 \text{ in} = 1.5 \text{ in}$ $0.5 \times 2 \text{ in} = 1 \text{ in}$ $0.5 \times 0.5 \text{ in} = 0.25 \text{ in}$

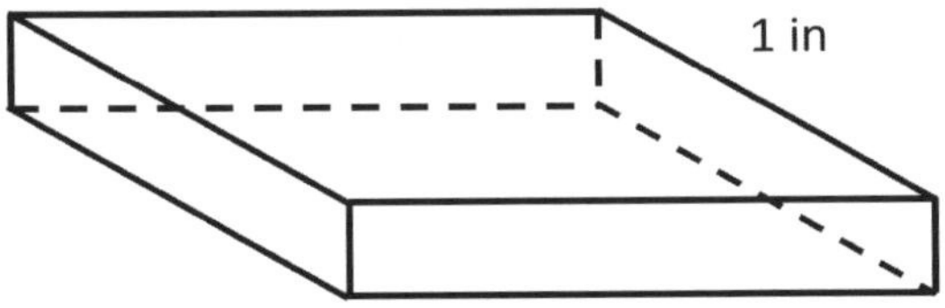


Since each side of the scale drawing is $\frac{1}{4}$ the size of each side of the actual box, the sides of the box are four times the size of the sides in the scale drawing. So, the box's actual dimensions are

- $4 \times 3 \text{ in} = 12 \text{ in}$ $4 \times 2 \text{ in} = 8 \text{ in}$ $4 \times 0.5 \text{ in} = 2 \text{ in}$.

### *Example*

The ratio of the lengths of two squares is 1:5.

- Determine the ratio of the perimeters of the two squares.
- Determine the ratio of the areas of the two squares.

If the ratio of the lengths of two squares is 1:5, the ratio of the perimeters of the two squares is also 1:5. Consider, for instance, a square with a length of 1 cm. Its width would also be 1 cm, so it perimeter would be $2l + 2w = 2(1 \text{ cm}) + 2(1 \text{ cm}) = 2 \text{ cm} + 2 \text{ cm} = 4 \text{ cm}$. A square with a length five times that of the first square would have a perimeter of $2(5 \text{ cm}) + 2(5 \text{ cm}) = 10 \text{ cm} + 10 \text{ cm} = 20 \text{ cm}$. So, the ratio of the perimeters of the squares would be 4:20, which reduces to 1:5.

Considering the same two squares, the area of the first square would be $l \times w = (1 \text{ cm})(1 \text{ cm}) = 1 \text{ cm}^2$. The area of the second would be $(5 \text{ cm})(5 \text{ cm}) = 25 \text{ cm}^2$. So, the ratios of the areas of the squares **would be 1:25.**

### *Example*

Determine whether or not a triangle can be constructed given

- The measures of three angles.
- The lengths of three sides.

The sum of the measures of a triangle's angles is always 180°. So, a triangle can be constructed from given angle measurements only if those measurements add to 180°.

The sum of the lengths of two shorter sides of a triangle must be greater than the length of the third side.

### *EXAMPLE*

Using a ruler and a protractor, draw a right triangle with the two shorter sides measuring 3 in and 4 in. Measure the length of the longest side and the approximate measures of the two non-right angles. Make sure the measurements are consistent with the properties of a triangle.

The length of the longest side is 5 inches. The angle across from the side measuring 4 inches is approximately 53°, and the other angle is approximately 37°. These measures are consistent with the properties of triangles:

- The sum of the angles of the triangle is $53° + 37° + 90° = 180°$. The combined lengths of the two shorter sides exceed the longest side: $3 \text{ in} + 4 \text{ in} > 5\ in$. The smallest angle forms the shortest side, and the largest angle forms the longest side.

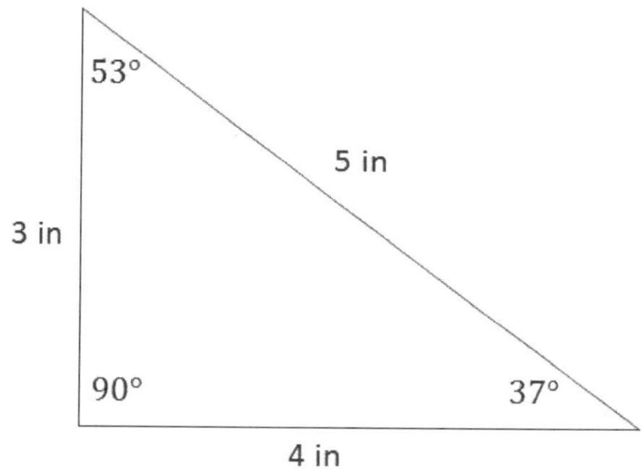


### *EXAMPLE*

An equilateral triangle whose sides each measure two inches is enlarged by a factor of four. Determine the measurements of the enlarged triangle's sides and angles.

A triangle which has three congruent sides also must have three congruent angles. Since the sum of the angles of a triangle is 180°, each angle measures $\frac{180°}{3} = 60°$. When a triangle is dilated, its angles remain the same; the lengths of the sides change but remain proportionally. Since the scale factor is four, the length of each the three sides is $2 \text{ in} \times 4 = 8 \text{ in}$. So, each angle of the enlarged triangle measures 60°, and each side measures 8 in.

### EXAMPLE

The area, $A$, of a parallelogram can be found using the formula $A = bh$, where $b$ is the length of the base and $h$ is the height, which is the distance between the parallelogram's base and its opposite, parallel side. Two congruent triangles are obtained when a parallelogram is cut in half from one of its corners to the opposite corner. From this information, determine the area formula of a triangle.

Two identical triangles make up the parallelogram's area, so the area of one triangle is half the area of the parallelogram. Since the area of a parallelogram is $A = bh$, the area of a triangle is $A = \frac{1}{2}bh$, where $b$ is the base of the triangle and $h$ is the height of the triangle as shown.

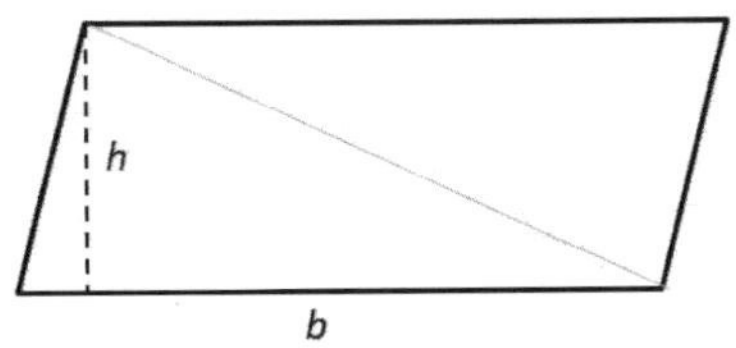


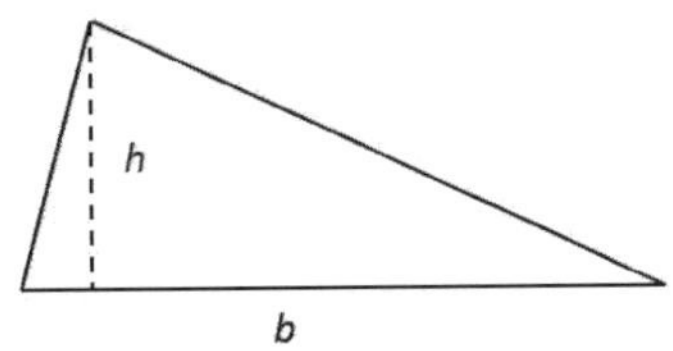


### EXAMPLE

Determine if no triangle, one triangle, or more than one triangle can be drawn given the side and/or angle measurements.

- Side lengths 3 cm, 4 cm, and 5 cm.
- Angle measurements 60°, 40°, and 80°.

In order to construct a triangle, the sum of the lengths of two shorter sides of a triangle must be greater than the length of the third side. $3 \text{ cm} + 4 \text{ cm} > 5\ cm$, so these sides can be used to draw one triangle.

The sum of the measures of a triangle's angles is always 180°. Since 60°+ 40°+ 80°=180°, a triangle can be constructed with these angle measurements. In fact, many similar triangles can be constructed with these angle measures.

### EXAMPLE

Determine the two-dimensional cross section obtained by slicing a right, triangular prism parallel to its base

A triangular prism contains two congruent triangular bases which lie in parallel planes. The side edges of a right prism are perpendicular to the base.

Taking the cross section of right, triangular prism parallel to its base yields a triangle which is congruent to the prism's base. One such cross section is illustrated.

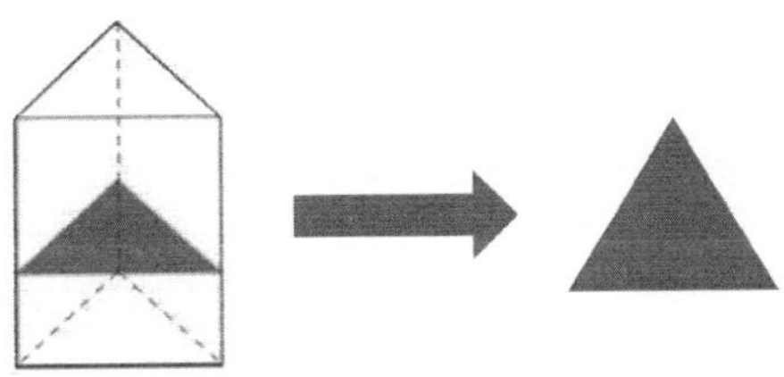

### EXAMPLE

Determine the two-dimensional cross section obtained by slicing a right, triangular prism perpendicular to its base

The cross section of right, triangular prism perpendicular to its base yields a rectangle. One such cross section is illustrated.

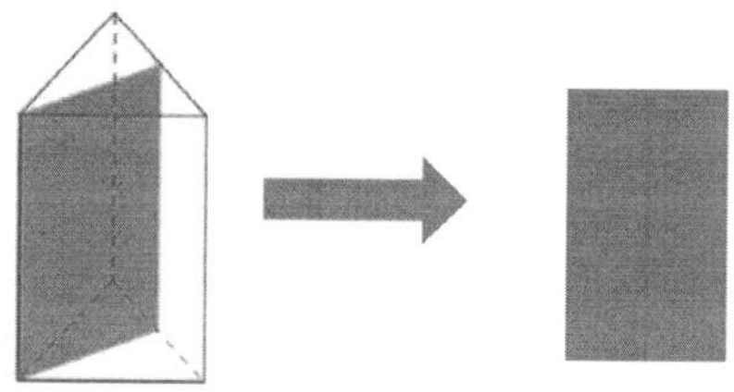

### EXAMPLE

Determine the two-dimensional cross section obtained by slicing a right, rectangular pyramid parallel to its base

A rectangular pyramid is one which has one rectangular base and four triangular sides which meet at an apex. The apex of a right pyramid lies directly above the center of the pyramid's base.

The cross section of a right, rectangular pyramid parallel to its base is a rectangle which is smaller than but similar to the rectangular base. One such cross section is illustrated.

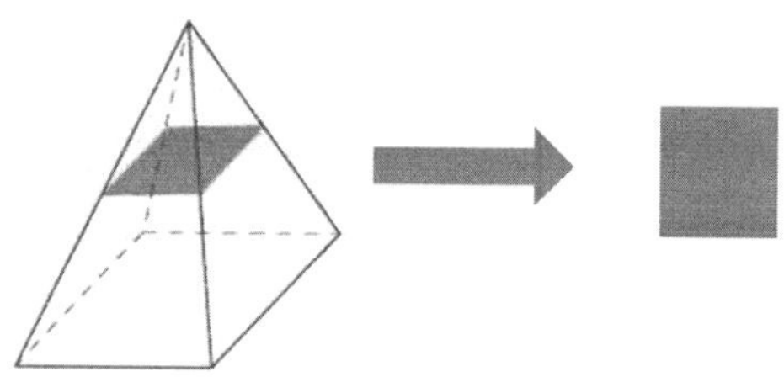

### EXAMPLE

Determine the two-dimensional cross section obtained by slicing a right, rectangular pyramid perpendicular to its base and through the apex.

A rectangular pyramid is one which has one rectangular base and four triangular sides which meet at an apex. The apex of a right pyramid lies directly above the center of the pyramid's base.

The cross section of a right, rectangular pyramid perpendicular to its base and through its apex is a triangle whose height is equal to the height of the pyramid. One such cross section is illustrated.

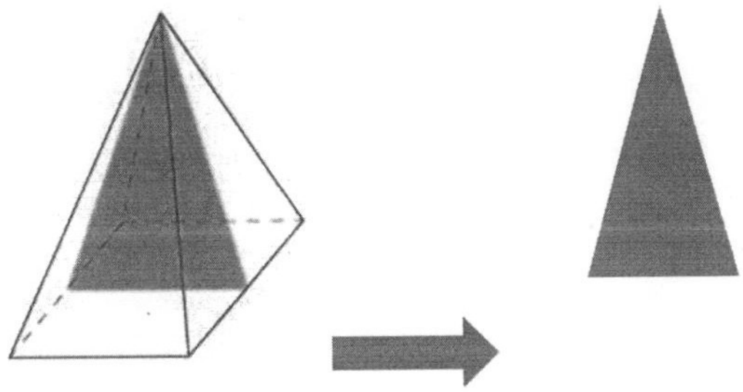

### *EXAMPLE*

Write the formulas used to find the circumference and area of a circle, respectively.

The formula used to find the circumference, $C$, of a circle is $C = 2\pi r$ or $C = \pi d$, where $r$ is the radius of the circle and $d$ its diameter. The formula used to find the area, A, of a circle is $A = \pi r^2$, where $r$ is the radius of the circle.

### *EXAMPLE*

A round table has a diameter of 6 feet. A circular table cloth is cut from a piece of fabric in such a way that it hangs down 6 inches all the way around the table, and a decorative fringe is added along the cut. Using 3.14 as an approximation for π, determine the area of the table cloth and the length of the fringe. Round answers to the nearest tenth.

The area of the table cloth is found using the area formula of a circle, $A = \pi r^2$. First, find the radius of the table cloth.

Since the table cloth hangs down 6", which is equivalent to half a foot, add 0.5 ft to the radius of the table to find the radius of the table cloth. The radius of the table cloth is 3.5 ft, so the area of the table cloth is about 38.5 square feet:

$$A = \pi r^2$$
$$A = (3.14)(3.5\text{ ft})^2$$
$$A = (3.14)(3.5\text{ ft})^2$$
$$A = (3.14)(12.25\text{ ft}^2) = 38.465\text{ ft}^2$$

The fringe goes around the circular table cloth, so its length can be found using the formula for the circumference of a circle, $C = 2\pi r$. The length of the fringe is about 22.0 ft.

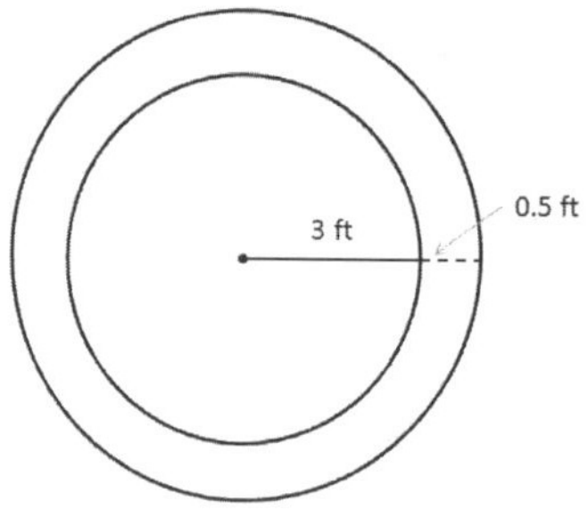


$$C = 2\pi r$$

$$C = 2(3.14)(3.5\text{ ft}) = 21.98\text{ ft}$$

### *EXAMPLE*

Name a pair of:

- Supplementary angles
- Complementary angles
- Vertical angles
- Adjacent angles

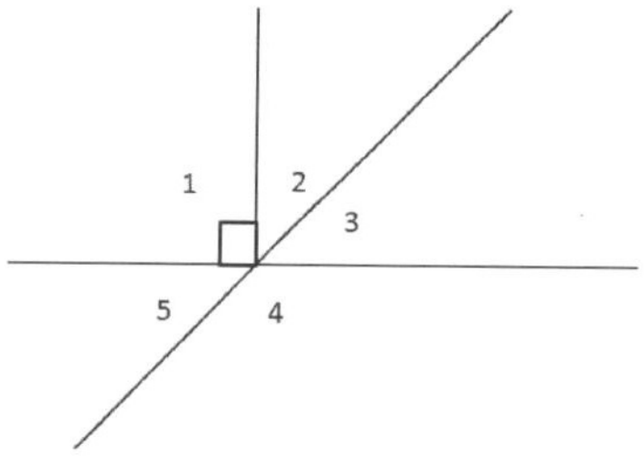


The sum of two supplementary angles is 180°. Angles 4 and 5 are supplementary, as are angles 3 and 4.

The sum of two complementary angles is 90°. Angles 2 and 3 are complimentary.

Vertical angles share a vertex but are not adjacent; rather, vertical angles are congruent angles across from each other in the X made by the intersection of two lines. Angles 3 and 5 are vertical angles.

Adjacent angles share a vertex and a side. Angles 1 and 2, 2 and 3, 3 and 4, 4 and 5, and 1 and 5 are adjacent.

Example

Solve for x and label each angle with its appropriate measure.

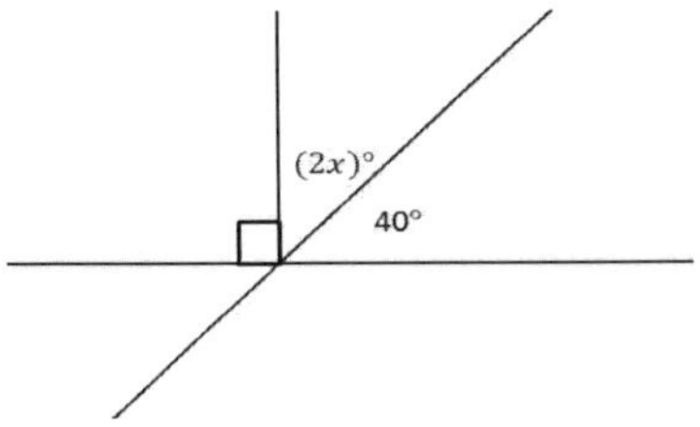


Since the angle labeled $(2x)°$ is the complement to the 40° angle, the two add to 90°. So,

$$\begin{aligned} 2x + 40 &= 90 \\ -40 &\quad -40 \\ 2x + 0 &= 50 \\ \frac{2x}{2} &= \frac{50}{2} \\ x &= 25 \end{aligned}$$

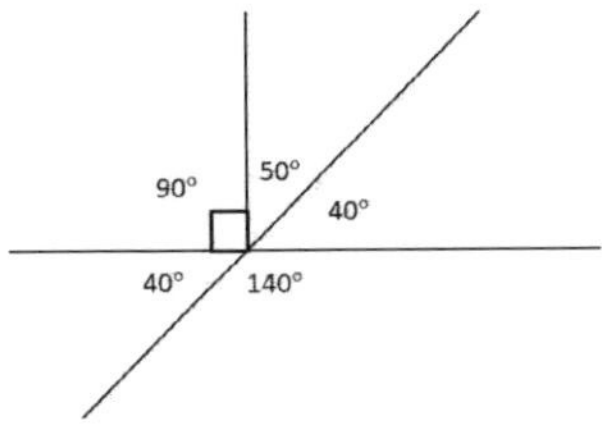


The angle labeled $(2x)°$ measures $(2\times25)° = 50°$.

The angle supplementary to the 40° angle must measure 140° since the sum of supplementary angles is 180°.

The angle across from the 40° angle is its vertical angle. Since vertical angles are congruent, that angle also measures 40°.

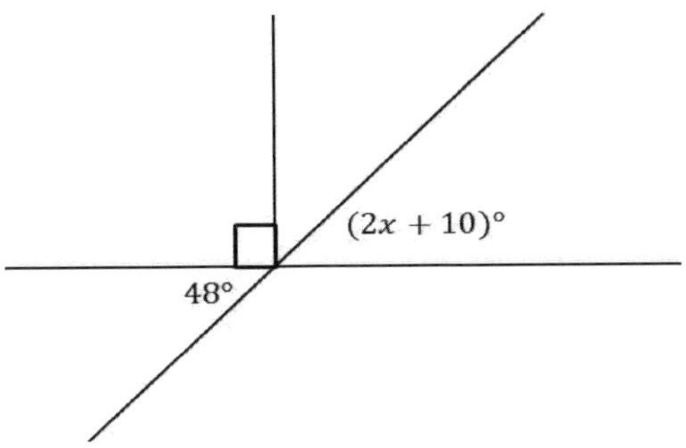


Since the angle labeled $(2x)°$ is the complement to the 40° angle, the two add to 90°. So,

$$\begin{aligned} 2x + 10 &= 48 \\ -10 &\quad -10 \\ 2x + 0 &= 38 \\ \frac{2x}{2} &= \frac{38}{2} \\ x &= 19 \end{aligned}$$

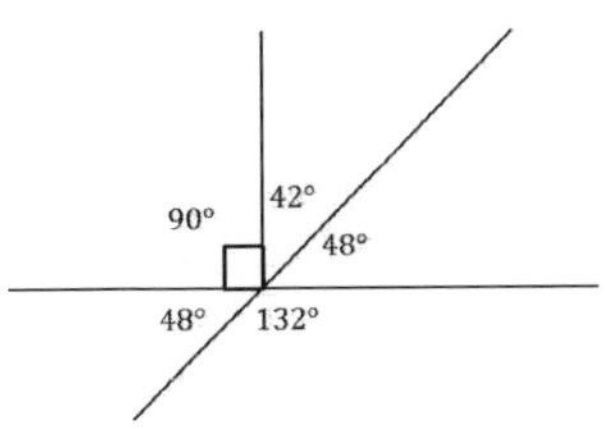

The angles label $(2x + 10)°$ measures 48°, so its complement measures $90° - 48° = 42°$, and its supplement measures $180° - 48° = 132°$.

### EXAMPLE

Match each measurement with the appropriate unit of measurement.

Length of a table
Area of a house
Perimeter of a room
Surface area of a polyhedron
Volume of a box
Distance between two houses
Storage capacity of a refrigerator

<u>Units</u>
Feet
Square feet
Cubic feet

Lengths or distances are measured in units, while area is measured is square units and volume is measured in cubic units. When the unit of measure is feet:

- The length of a table is measured in *feet.*
- The area of a house is measured in *square feet.*
- The perimeter of a room is the distance around the room and is measured in *feet.*
- The surface area of a polyhedron is the sum of the areas of its polygonal faces and is measured in *square feet.*
- The volume of a box is measured in *cubic feet.*
- The distance between two houses is measured in *feet.*
- The storage capacity of a refrigerator is how much space is inside. The refrigerator's volume is measured in *cubic feet.*

### EXAMPLE

Find the surface area and volume of the box.

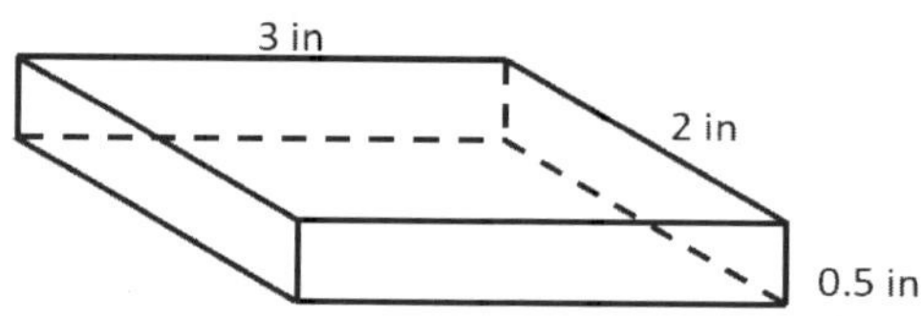


The surface area of a box is the sum of the areas of its six rectangular surfaces.

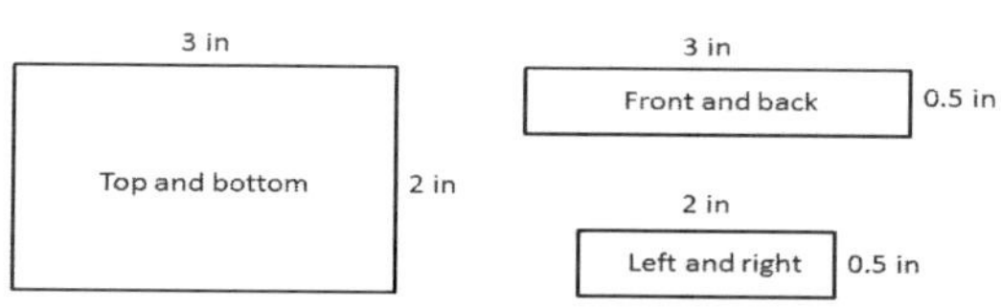


The area of the top rectangle is $A = lw = (3 \text{ in})(2 \text{ in}) = 6 \text{ in}^2$. The area of the top rectangle combined with the bottom rectangle is $6 \text{ in}^2 + 6 \text{ in}^2 = 12 \text{ in}^2$.

The area of the front rectangle is $A = lw = (3 \text{ in})(0.5 \text{ in}) = 1.5 \text{ in}^2$. The area of the front rectangle combined with the back rectangle is $1.5 \text{ in}^2 + 1.5 \text{ in}^2 = 3 \text{ in}^2$.

The area of the left side rectangle is $A = lw = (2 \text{ in})(0.5 \text{ in}) = 1 \text{ in}^2$. The area of the left and right side rectangles together is $1 \text{ in}^2 + 1 \text{ in}^2 = 2 \text{ in}^2$.

The total surface area of the box is $12\ in^2 + 3\ in^2 +\ 2\ in^2 = 17\ in^2$.

The volume, $V$, of a box is found by $V = lwh$. o, $V = (3\ in)(2in)(0.5\ in) = 3\ in^3$.

### EXAMPLE

An 11'×13' room contains a 3' wide, 7' tall doorway and two 5'x3' windows. The ceiling height is 9'. Determine :

- The price to install baseboards which cost \$1.25 per linear foot.
- The price to install flooring which costs \$5 per square foot.
- If one gallon of paint which covers 400 square feet of surface is sufficient to paint the walls of the room.

Baseboards run along the edge of the room, but not across doorways. To determine the price for the baseboards, first determine how many feet are needed for the perimeter of the room, excluding the doorway. Use the formula for the perimeter of a rectangle to find the perimeter of the room: $2l + 2w = 2(11 \text{ ft}) + 2(13 \text{ ft}) = 48 \text{ ft}$. After adjusting for the width of the doorway, 45ft of baseboard is needed for the room. The price of baseboards is 45×1.25=\$56.25.

To determine the price for flooring, first determine the area of the room. Use the formula for the area of a rectangle to find the area of the room: $lw = (11 \text{ ft})(13 \text{ ft}) = 143 \text{ ft}^2$. The price for the flooring is 143×5=\$715.

To determine the amount of paint needed for the walls, first determine the total surface area to be covered. Two walls are 11'×9' and the other two walls are 13'×9'. Disregarding doors and windows, the total area of the walls is $2(11 \text{ ft})(9 \text{ ft}) + 2(13 \text{ ft})(9 \text{ ft}) = 198 \text{ ft}^2 + 234 \text{ ft}^2 = 432 \text{ ft}^2$. Take away the area of the door, which is $(3 \text{ ft})(7 \text{ ft}) = 21 \text{ ft}^2$ , and the area of the windows, which is$2(5 \text{ ft})(3 \text{ ft}) = 30 \text{ ft}^2$: $432 \text{ ft}^2 - 21 \text{ ft}^2 - 30 \text{ ft}^2 = 381 \text{ ft}^2$. The amount of surface which needs paint is $381 \text{ ft}^2$. Purchasing one gallon of paint should be sufficient to cover the walls if only one coat of paint is needed.

### EXAMPLE

Find the perimeter of the shape below.

The perimeter of a polygon is the sum of its sides, which is 12 inches.

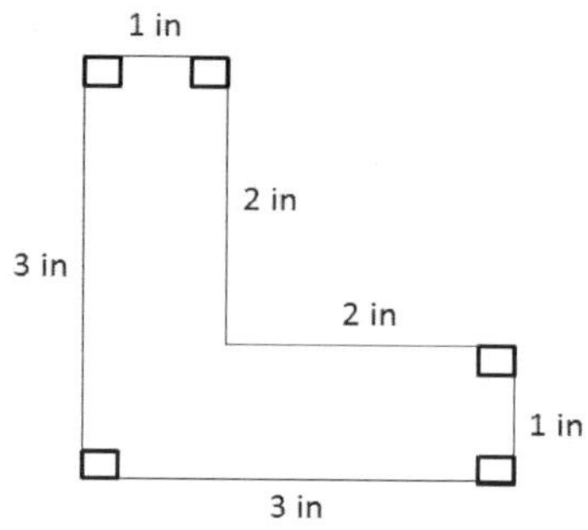


### EXAMPLE

Find the area of the shape below.

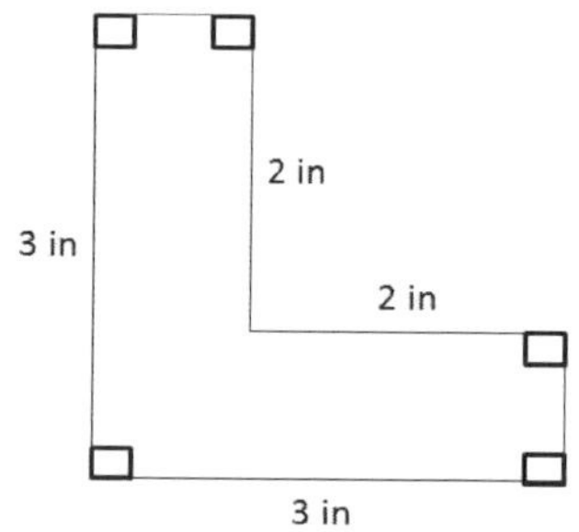


To find the area of an irregular polygon, draw it as a familiar polygon to which another familiar polygon is added or from which a familiar polygon is removed. For example, the shape can be viewed as vertically-oriented rectangle to which a horizontally-oriented rectangle is added, or it can be viewed as a square from which a smaller square is removed.

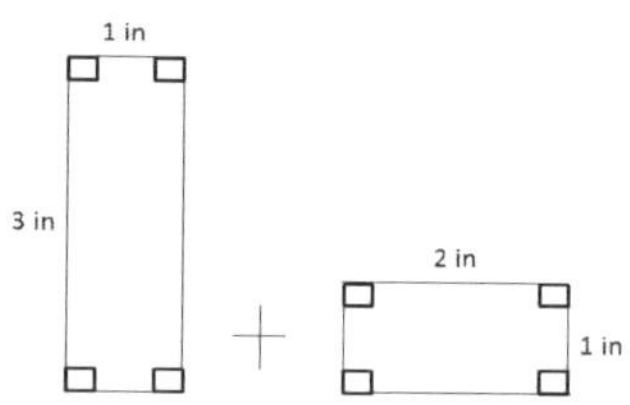


The area of the irregular polygon is the sum of the areas of the two rectangles shown. The area of a rectangle is $A = lw$, so the area of the polygon is $(3 \text{ in})(1 \text{ in}) + (2 \text{ in})(1 \text{ in}) = 3 \text{ in}^2 + 2 \text{ in}^2 = 5 \text{ in}^2$.

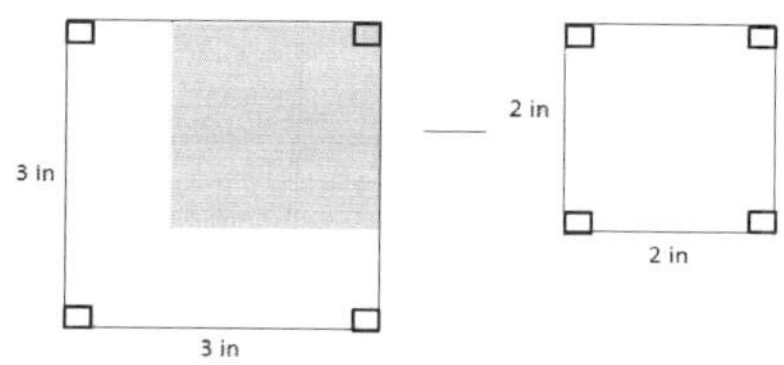


The area of the irregular polygon is the area of the larger square minus the area of the smaller square. The larger square has side lengths of 3 inches, so the area is $(3 \text{ in})(3 \text{ in}) = 9 \text{ in}^2$. The smaller square has an area of $4 \text{ in}^2$. So, the area of the irregular polygon is $9 \text{ in}^2 - 4 \text{ in}^2 = 5 \text{ in}^2$.

Notice that either method of calculating the irregular polygon's area gives the same answer.

## MEAN, MEDIAN, AND MODE

Mean, median, and mode are all measures of central tendency. Measures of central tendency summarize a set of data with values which represent the average, middle, or most common value. The mean, or average, of numerical data can be found by dividing the sum of the numbers in a set by how many numbers are in that set. When numerical data are organized from least to greatest, the middle number or average of the two middle numbers is the median of the set. The mode is the value which appears most frequently in a data set; there may be no mode, one mode, or more than one mode in a set.

### *EXAMPLE*

Find the mean, median, and mode of these numbers:

23, 42, 36, 21, 28, 29, 32, 28, 40, 36, 39.

The mean of a set of numbers is the sum of the numbers divided by how many numbers are in the set. So, the mean of this set of numbers is $\frac{23+42+36+21+28+29+32+28+40+36+39}{11} = \frac{354}{11} = 32.\overline{18}$.

To find the median, put the numbers in increasing order and find the number in the middle:

21, 23, 28, 28, 29, **32**, 36, 36, 39, 40, 42. The median is 32.

The mode is the value in the set that occurs most frequently. There may be no mode, one mode, or more than one mode in a set. This set has two values that occur twice while all others occur only once. Thus, the modes are those two values, namely 28 and 36.

## RANDOM SAMPLING

A random sample is a collection of members, chosen at random and with equal likelihood, from a group about which information is desired. Rather than collecting information from the entire group, which can be quite difficult when the group is very large, information is collected instead from the sample. If the sample is representative of the group and is sufficiently large, then the information gained from the sample is representative can be used to describe the group as a whole.

### *EXAMPLE*

Determine whether or not each represents a random sample of seventh graders at a middle school:

- A student selects all the seventh graders on her bus.
- A teacher puts the names of her first period students in a hat and draws ten names.
- A principal assigns uses a random number generator to select student ID numbers of seventh graders.

Each seventh grader must be chosen at random and must have an equal chance of being selected. Neither criterion is true in the first scenario. The teacher in the second scenario is selecting a random sample of students in her first period class, but this is not a random sample of the group of seventh graders as a whole. The principle's method of selecting is random and ensures that the likelihood of selecting one student is the same as the likelihood of selecting another.

### *EXAMPLE*

A random number generator produced the following sets of eight numbers between 1 and 99:

82, 60, 40, 69, 40, 36, 25, 59
98, 28, 15, 91, 51, 74, 11, 36
21, 66, 46, 16, 32, 73, 3, 81
91, 80, 32, 72, 1, 53, 51, 28.

Determine the mean of each set. Describe how well the mean of the each random sample represents the set from which the sample was taken.

The mean, or average, is a measure of central tendency which can be found by dividing the sum of the numbers in a set by how many numbers are in that set. The mean of the numbers 1 through 99 is 50, so the mean of a random sample of numbers taken from 1 to 99 should be approximately 50.

$$\frac{82+60+40+69+40+36+25+59}{8} = \frac{411}{8} = 51.375$$
$$\frac{98+28+15+91+51+74+11+36}{8} = \frac{404}{8} = 50.5$$
$$\frac{21+66+46+16+32+73+3+81}{9} = \frac{338}{8} = 42.25$$
$$\frac{91+80+32+72+1+53+51+28}{8} = \frac{408}{8} = 51$$

Samples 1, 2, and 4 seem to be a good representatives of the set from which they were taken. The mean of the values in the third sample varies more from the actual mean than the others. One way to improve the likelihood of a random sample's representation of the actual set is to collect more samples.

### *EXAMPLE*

Suppose all 567 seventh graders in a school vote on which field trip they would like to take from the following options: science center, art museum, or state capitol. Explain how an administrator might use the surveys to predict the most popular vote without tallying all of the results.

An administrator could compile the results from a random sample of surveys. For instance, if the surveys were shuffled, and 50 randomly chosen surveys showed a strong preference for the science center, then the administrator would likely predict that the science center will be the popular vote. To increase her confidence in the results, the administrator could increase the sample size by examining more surveys.

### *EXAMPLE*

When determining the reading level of a book, a publisher considers many factors, including the average word length. Explain how a publisher might use random sampling to find the average word length in a book.

To find the average word length in a book, a publisher might randomly select a set of words from the book and find the average length of those words. This average should be representative of the whole book if the words are indeed chosen at random.

### EXAMPLE

The histogram below displays the heights of randomly selected eighteen-year-old boys and girls living in Atlanta, Georgia. Compare the variability within each group and between the groups.

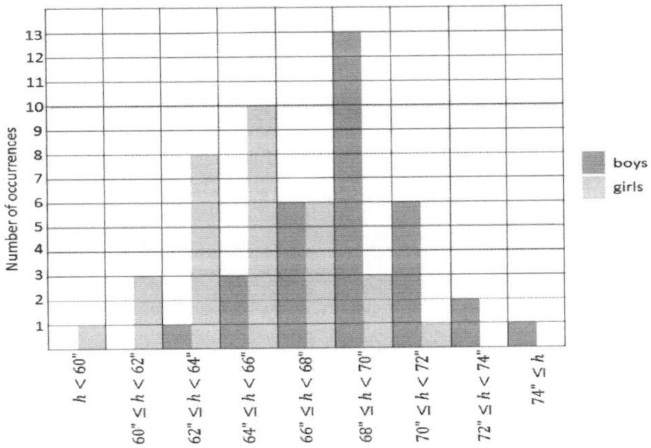


Both of the histograms show a similar, normal distribution of heights, with fewer individuals at the two extremes and the majority clustered at a more central point. The two distributions overlap, which means that some eighteen-year-old boys are the same height as some eighteen-year-old girls. However, there is a noticeable shift to the right in the bell-shaped distributions for boys when compared to girls; this indicates that eighteen-year-old boys are generally taller than girls of the same age. According to the chart, the most common height for eighteen-year-old boys is between 68 and 70 inches, while the most common height among girls is 64 and 66 inches.

## EXPLAIN WHAT EACH OF THE PROBABILITIES MEANS IN TERMS OF THE LIKELIHOOD OF AN EVENT:

$$0$$
$$\frac{1}{100,000}$$
$$\frac{1}{2}$$
$$99\%$$
$$1$$

The probability of an event occurring ranges from 0 to 1 when expressed as a fraction or decimal and between 0% and 100% when expressed as a percentage. When there are a finite number of outcomes, a probability of 0 means that the occurrence of an event is impossible, while a probability of 1 means the occurrence is certain. The closer a value is to 0, the less likely it is to occur. For example, a probability of $\frac{1}{100,000}$ indicates that an event is unlikely to occur, whereas a probability of 99% indicates a likely event. Since ½ is halfway between 0 and 1, a probability of ½, or 50%, means that an event is neither likely nor unlikely.

### In Terms of Probability, Define and Give an Example of a

- Sample space
- Simple event
- Compound event

The set of all outcomes of a probability experiment is called the sample space. For example, if a coin is tossed one time, there are two possible outcomes: heads or tails. So, the sample space consists of two elements. If a coin is tossed two times, there are four possible outcomes: heads then tails, heads then heads, tails then heads, tails then tails. So, the sample space consists of four outcomes.

A simple event consists of only one outcome in the sample space. For instance, the event of getting heads in a single coin toss is a simple event.

Compound events consist of more than one outcome in the sample space. For instance, the event of getting heads at least once in two coin tosses is a compound event. The compound event of getting heads is composed of three outcomes: heads then tails, heads then heads, tails then heads.

### Determine the Following:

- The probability of winning a single coin toss.
- The probability of a rolling a multiple of 3 on a die.
- The probability of randomly picking a green marble from a bag containing 15 blue marbles and 5 green marbles.
- The probability of randomly picking a red marble from a bag containing 15 blue marbles and 5 green marbles.

Probability is the chance that something will happen. The probability of an event is the ratio of the number of favorable outcomes to the number of possible outcomes when all outcomes are equally likely.

Because there is one favorable outcome of two equally likely outcomes, so the probability of winning a coin toss is ½, or 50%.

Both 3 and 6 are multiples of 3, so there are two favorable outcomes out of six equally likely total outcomes. So, the probability of rolling a multiple of 3 on a die is $\frac{2}{6} = \frac{1}{3} = 33.\bar{3}\%$.

There are five green marbles and fifteen blue marbles in a bag. The probability of picking a green marble is the ratio of green marbles to total marbles, or $\frac{5}{20} = \frac{1}{4} = 25\%$.

Because there are no red marbles in the bag, it is not possible to choose a red marble from the bag. Therefore, the probability of choosing a red marble is 0.

### Distinguish Between Theoretical Probability and Experimental Probability.

Theoretical probability is the expected likelihood of an event. Experimental probability is found by conducting trials and comparing the actual occurrence of an event to the number of trials.

For example, the probability of rolling a 2 on a die is 1/6 because there is one favorable outcome, namely rolling a 2, and six equally possible outcomes. So, theoretically, a 2 would appear 100 times if a die is rolled 600 times. Suppose, however, that a die is actually rolled 600 times, and a 2 appears 90 times. The experimental probability is $\frac{90}{600} = \frac{3}{20}$.

If the die is a fair die, the experimental probability should closely approximate or equal the theoretical probability when many trials are conducted.

### DETERMINE THE PROBABILITY THAT THE SPINNER WILL LAND ON BLACK AND PREDICT THE NUMBER OF TIMES THE SPINNER WILL LAND ON BLACK IF THE SPINNER IS SPUN 100 TIMES.

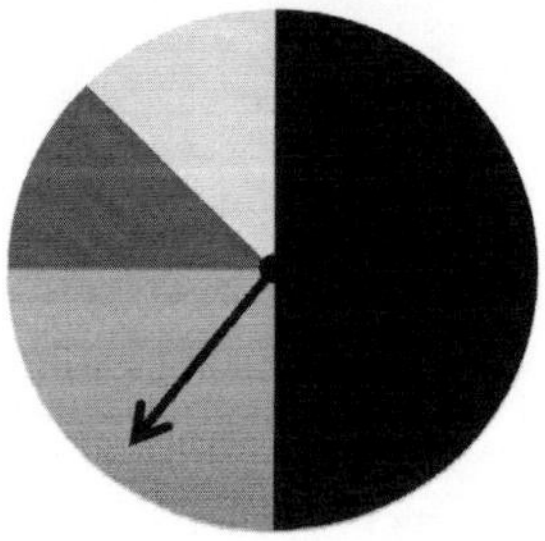

The probabilities of different outcomes on the spinner are not equally likely. Notice that the black section comprises half the circle. So, the spinner will *probably* land in the black section half the time. So, out of 100 spins, the spinner will land in the black section *about* 50 times.

### EXAMINE THE DATA COLLECTED FROM 100 COIN TOSSES. DETERMINE THE EXPERIMENTAL PROBABILITY OF THIS TOSSED COIN LANDING ON HEADS (H).

| H | H | T | H | T | T | H | T | H | T |
|---|---|---|---|---|---|---|---|---|---|
| T | T | H | T | H | H | T | H | H | T |
| H | H | T | T | T | T | H | H | T | H |
| T | H | T | H | H | T | H | H | T | T |
| H | H | T | H | T | T | H | H | H | T |
| H | T | T | T | H | H | T | H | T | T |
| H | T | H | H | T | H | T | T | H | T |
| H | T | H | H | T | H | T | H | H | T |
| H | H | T | T | H | T | H | H | T | H |
| T | T | H | T | H | H | T | T | T | H |

Out of 100 trials, 51 coin flips landed on heads, so the experimental probability of getting heads in a coin toss is 51/100. This is very close to the predicted outcome of 50 heads from 100 tosses based on the theoretical probability that a coin will land on heads ($\frac{1}{2}$, or 50%).

### THE RESULTS OF 24 ROLLS OF A DIE ARE TABULATED BELOW. DETERMINE WHETHER OR NOT THE RESULTS ARE CONSISTENT WITH THE EXPECTED RESULTS AND EXPLAIN POSSIBLE REASONS FOR A DISCREPANCY IF ONE EXISTS.

| | 1 | 2 | 3 | 4 | 5 | 6 |
|---|---|---|---|---|---|---|
| **Number of times rolled** | 3 | 4 | 8 | 3 | 2 | 4 |

The results of the experiment are not consistent with the expected results. This could be because the die is "loaded" or because enough trials were not performed in the experiment. To determine whether or not the die is loaded, conduct more trials and see if the results are consistent with the expected results based on the experimental probability seen here.

| | 1 | 2 | 3 | 4 | 5 | 6 |
|---|---|---|---|---|---|---|
| **Number of times rolled** | 3 | 4 | 8 | 3 | 2 | 4 |
| **Experiment al probability** | $\frac{3}{24}=\frac{1}{8}$ | $\frac{4}{24}=\frac{1}{6}$ | $\frac{8}{24}=\frac{1}{3}$ | $\frac{3}{24}=\frac{1}{8}$ | $\frac{2}{24}=\frac{1}{12}$ | $\frac{4}{24}=\frac{1}{6}$ |
| **Theoretical probability** | $\frac{1}{6}$ | $\frac{1}{6}$ | $\frac{1}{6}$ | $\frac{1}{6}$ | $\frac{1}{6}$ | $\frac{1}{6}$ |
| **Expected results** $\mathbf{\frac{1}{6}\times\frac{24}{1}=\frac{24}{6}=4}$ | 4 | 4 | 4 | 4 | 4 | 4 |

**The results of 24 rolls of a die are tabulated below. Determine the experimental probability from these results and use it to predict the number of times each result will occur if a number cube is rolled 200 times.**

| | 1 | 2 | 3 | 4 | 5 | 6 |
|---|---|---|---|---|---|---|
| **Number of times rolled** | 3 | 4 | 8 | 3 | 2 | 4 |

The predicted results of 200 rolls based on the experimental probabilities are shown below.

| | 1 | 2 | 3 | 4 | 5 | 6 |
|---|---|---|---|---|---|---|
| **Number of times rolled** | 200 | 200 | 200 | 200 | 200 | 200 |
| **Experimental probability** | $\frac{1}{8}$ | $\frac{1}{6}$ | $\frac{1}{3}$ | $\frac{1}{8}$ | $\frac{1}{12}$ | $\frac{1}{6}$ |
| **Predicted results** | $\frac{200}{8}=25$ | $\frac{200}{6}\approx 33$ | $\frac{200}{3}\approx 67$ | $\frac{200}{8}=25$ | $\frac{200}{12}\approx 17$ | $\frac{200}{6}\approx 33$ |

Note that every predicted result is rounded to the nearest whole number since there cannot exist a fraction of a roll. Check to makesure the sum of the rounded numbers is 200: 25+33+67+25+17+33=200.

If the die is indeed loaded, these would be the predicted results. If the die is fair, the results of 200 rolls should show an even distribution of around 33 or 34 rolls over all outcomes.

**Joseph is in a math class with 23 other students, 14 of whom are girls. If a student is selected at random from the class, determine the probability that:**

- The student selected is Joseph.
- The student selected is a boy.

Since each student has an equally likely chance of being selected from the class, the probability of selecting Joseph is $\frac{1}{number\ of\ students\ in\ the\ class}$. The number of students in the class, including Joseph, is 24. So, $P(\text{Joseph}) = \frac{1}{24}$.

Since each student has an equally likely chance of being selected from the class, the probability of selecting a boy is $\frac{number\ of\ boys\ in\ the\ class}{number\ of\ students\ in\ the\ class}$. Since 14 of the 24 students are girls, there are 10 boys. So, $P(boy) = \frac{10}{24} = \frac{5}{12}$.

**A baby inherited one copy of a beta-globin gene from her mother and one from her father. Both the baby's mother and father are carriers for sickle cell anemia, meaning that each parent contains a normal allele for beta-globin called type A, and a recessive allele which has a single mutation called type S. The Punnet square below shows the possible genotypes (types of genes) and phenotypes (expressions of the genotypes). Determine the probability that the baby has sickle cell anemia. Express the probabilities as a fraction and as a percent.**

| | A | S |
|---|---|---|
| A | AA (no disease) | AS (no disease/carrier) |
| S | AS (no disease/carrier) | SS (sickle cell anemia) |

The probability that the baby will have sickle cell anemia is ¼, or 25%.

| | A | S |
|---|---|---|
| A | AA (no disease) | AS (no disease/carrier) |
| a | AS (no disease/carrier) | SS (sickle cell anemia) |

**DETERMINE THE PROBABILITY THAT THE BABY HAS INHERITED A MUTATED ALLELE FROM AT LEAST ONE OF HER PARENTS. EXPRESS THE PROBABILITIES AS A FRACTION AND AS A PERCENT.**

| | A | S |
|---|---|---|
| A | AA (no disease) | AS (no disease/carrier) |
| S | AS (no disease/carrier) | SS (sickle cell anemia) |

The probability that the baby has inherited a mutated allele from at least one of her parents is ¾, or 75%.

| | A | S |
|---|---|---|
| A | AA (no disease) | AS (no disease/carrier) |
| a | AS (no disease/carrier) | SS (sickle cell anemia) |

**Determine the probability that the baby does not have the disease but carries one copy of the mutated allele. Express the probabilities as a fraction and as a percent.**

| | A | S |
|---|---|---|
| A | AA (no disease) | AS (no disease/carrier) |
| S | AS (no disease/carrier) | SS (sickle cell anemia) |

The probability that the baby does not have the disease but carries one copy of the mutated allele is $\frac{2}{4} = \frac{1}{2}$, or 50%.

| | A | S |
|---|---|---|
| **A** | AA (no disease) | AS (no disease/carrier) |
| **a** | AS (no disease/carrier) | SS (sickle cell anemia) |

**Show the sample space for rolling two dice and find the probability of rolling double sixes.**

Since there are six outcomes for each die, there are $6 \times 6 = 36$ outcomes for rolling two dice.

| 1,1 | 1,2 | 1,3 | 1,4 | 1,5 | 1,6 |
|---|---|---|---|---|---|
| 2,1 | 2,2 | 2,3 | 2,4 | 2,5 | 2,6 |
| 3,1 | 3,2 | 3,3 | 3,4 | 3,5 | 3,6 |
| 4,1 | 4,2 | 4,3 | 4,4 | 4,5 | 4,6 |
| 5,1 | 5,2 | 5,3 | 5,4 | 5,5 | 5,6 |
| 6,1 | 6,2 | 6,3 | 6,4 | 6,5 | 6,6 |

For fair dice, each outcome is equally likely. So, the probability can be found $\frac{number\ of\ double\ sixes}{number\ of\ outcomes}$

Only one of the 36 possible outcomes is double sixes, so the probability of getting double sixes is $\frac{1}{36}$.

USE A TREE DIAGRAM TO DETERMINE THE PROBABILITY THAT OF TWO CARDS PULLED FROM TWO DIFFERENT DECKS, AT LEAST ONE IS A HEART.

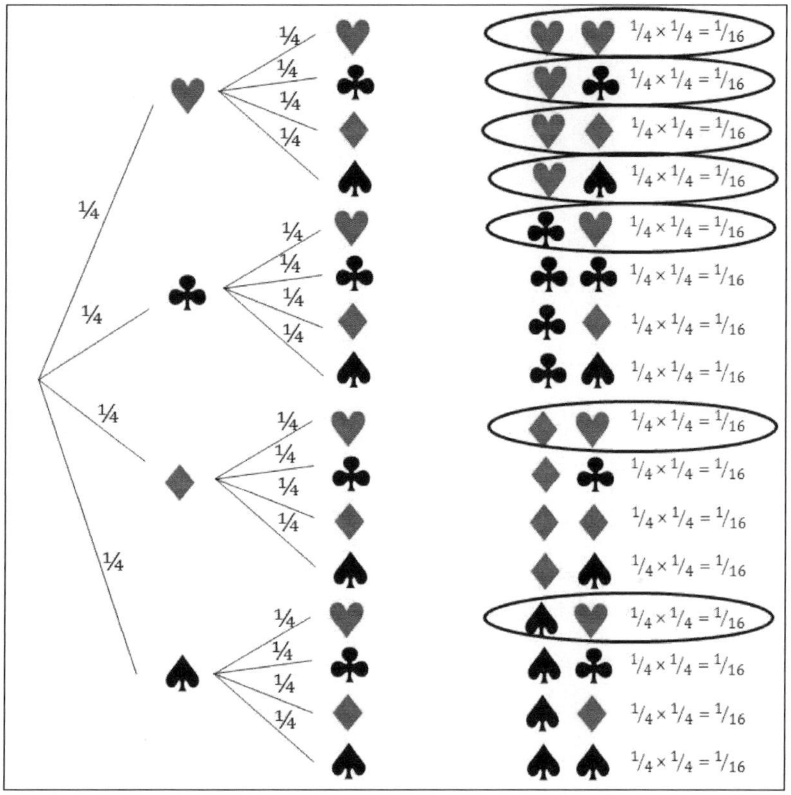

The probability of getting at least one heart includes the outcomes in which a heart is selected from the first deck, in which a heart is selected from the second deck, and in which a heart is selected from both decks. Seven of the sixteen outcomes include at least one heart, so the probability that at least one of the two cards drawn is a heart is $\frac{7}{16}$.

USE A TREE DIAGRAM TO DETERMINE THE PROBABILITY THAT TWO CARDS PULLED FROM TWO DIFFERENT DECKS ARE BOTH SPADES.

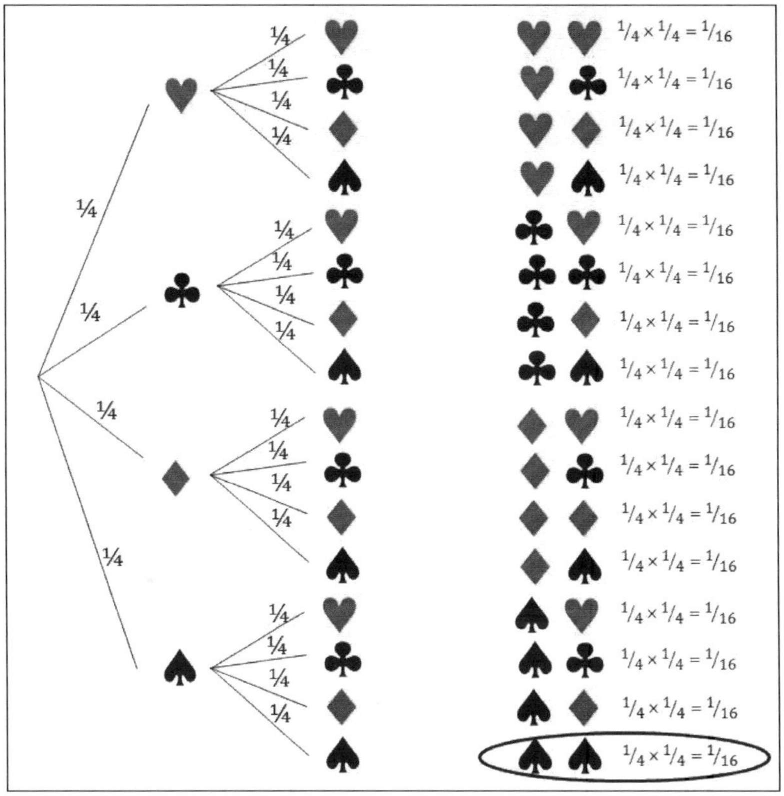

One out of sixteen outcomes is drawing a spade from both decks. So, the probability that both cards are spades is $\frac{1}{16}$.

Notice that the probability of each outcome in the sample space can be found by multiplying the probability of the first event by the probability of the second event.

SUPPOSE A COUPLE HAS A ¼ CHANCE OF HAVING A CHILD WITH SICKLE CELL ANEMIA. EXPLAIN WHETHER OR NOT EACH STATEMENT IS TRUE.

- If the couple's first child has sickle cell anemia, then their second child will not have sickle cell anemia.
- If the couple has eight children, two of them will have sickle cell anemia.
- If the couple has six children, it is unlikely that all of them will have sickle cell anemia.

The statement *If the couple's first child has sickle cell anemia, then their second child will not have sickle cell anemia* is **not necessarily true**. If a couple's first child is affected, it is possible for second child to have the disease, too. Each child conceived by the couple has a ¼ chance of developing the disease. The fact that the first child has the disease has no effect on the second child's chance of having it.

The statement *If a couple has eight children, two of them will have sickle cell anemia* is **not necessarily true**. You can predict based on the probability that one in four of the couple's children will be affected that, of eight children, two will have the disease. However, it is possible that none, all, or any number of the children will have the disease.

The statement *If the couple has six children, it is unlikely that all of them will have sickle cell anemia* is **true**. This statement mentions only the relative likelihood of an occurrence. The probability that all six children would have the disease is $\frac{1}{4} \times \frac{1}{4} \times \frac{1}{4} \times \frac{1}{4} \times \frac{1}{4} \times \frac{1}{4} = \frac{1}{4096}$. A probability of $\frac{1}{4096}$ indicates that is unlikely for all six children to have the disease.

# Mathematics Practice Test #1

## Practice Questions

**1. Ana has completed approximately $\frac{2}{7}$ of her research paper. Which of the following best represents the percentage of the paper she has completed?**

a. 24%
b. 26%
c. 27%
d. 29%

**2. Simplify the expression: $2n + (3n - 2)^2$**

_______________________________________________

**3. Elijah has prepared $2\frac{1}{2}$ gallons of lemonade to distribute to guests at a party. If there are 25 guests, how much lemonade is available to each guest, given that each guest receives an equal amount?**

a. $\frac{1}{8}$ of a gallon
b. $\frac{1}{6}$ of a gallon
c. $\frac{1}{12}$ of a gallon
d. $\frac{1}{10}$ of a gallon

**4. The points M, N, and O are plotted on the number line below. Plot point P based on the equation: $N - M + O = P$**

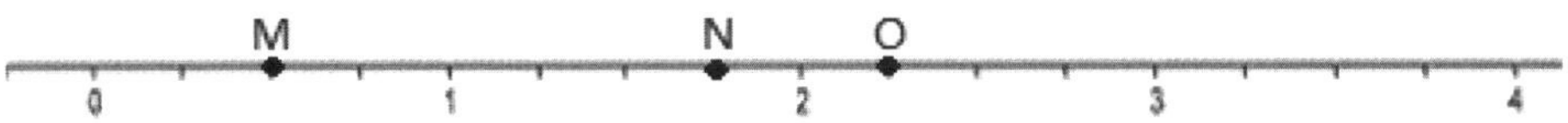


**5. Part A: Edward spins the spinner below three times. If the spinner lands on a different number each time what is the highest total he could get?**

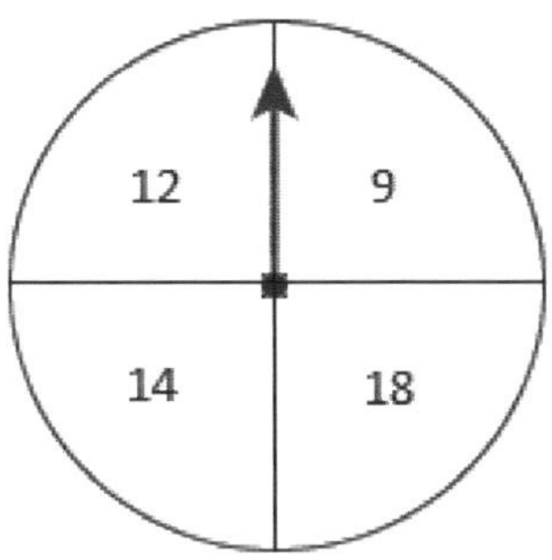


_______________________________________________

**Part B: He decides to spin it one more time. What is the probability that he will land on a number that he has already landed on?**

____________________________________

**6. A bag of coffee costs \$9.85 and contains 16 ounces of coffee. Which of the following best represents the cost per ounce?**

a. \$0.67
b. \$0.64
c. \$0.65
d. \$0.62

**7. Which of the following is equivalent to $4^3 + 12 \div 4 + 8^2 \times 3$?**

a. 249
b. 393
c. 211
d. 259

**8. Part A: The ingredients needed for a cake are given below:**

- 2 eggs
- $1\frac{3}{4}$ cups of flour
- 2 teaspoons baking soda
- ½ cup butter
- $1\frac{1}{4}$ teaspoons vanilla extract
- $\frac{3}{4}$ cup of milk

**What is the ratio of butter to flour?**

a. 1:3
b. 2:5
c. 2:7
d. 3:2

**Part B: When Lucy is making the cake she accidently puts a whole cup of milk in it. What was the ratio of milk to flour before and what is it now?**

__________________________ __________________________

**9. Part A: The original price of a jacket is \$36.95. The jacket is discounted by 25%. Before tax, which of the following best represents the cost of the jacket?**

a. \$27.34
b. \$27.71
c. \$28.82
d. \$29.56

**Part B: If tax is 8% how much does it cost?**

__________________________________

**10. Martin and his friends are taking a road trip from Houston, TX to Las Vegas, NV. The trip will take two days and they will spend the night in El Paso, TX. The first day they drove for 11 hours at a rate of 69 miles per hour. The next day they drove for 10 hours at a rate of 72 miles per hour. How far is it from Houston to Las Vegas?**

______________________________

**11. A bottle of lotion contains 20 fluid ounces and costs $3.96. Which of the following best represents the cost per fluid ounce?**

a. $0.18
b. $0.20
c. $0.22
d. $0.24

**12. Solve the equation for x: $3^2 + 2x = 17$.**

______________________________

**13. Given the figure below what is the area of the shaded regions? Figure is not to scale.**

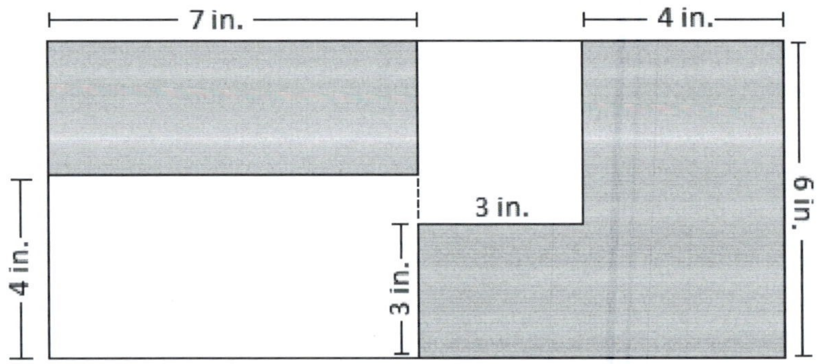


______________________________

**14. Given the sequence represented in the table below, where *n* represents the position of the term and $a_n$ represents the value of the term, which of the following describes the relationship between the position number and the value of the term?**

| n | 1 | 2 | 3 | 4 | 5 | 6 |
|---|---|---|---|---|---|---|
| $a_n$ | 5 | 2 | −1 | −4 | −7 | −10 |

a. Multiply *n* by 2 and subtract 4
b. Multiply *n* by 2 and subtract 3
c. Multiply *n* by −3 and add 8
d. Multiply *n* by −4 and add 1

**15. The number 123 is the 11th term in a sequence with a constant rate of change. Which of the following sequences has this number as its 11th term?**

a. 5, 17, 29, 41, ...
b. 3, 15, 27, 39, ...
c. −1, 11, 23, 35, ...
d. 1, 13, 25, 37, ...

16. **Kevin pays \$12.95 for a text messaging service plus \$0.07 for each text message he sends. Which of the following equations could be used to represent the total cost, $y$, when $x$ represents the number of text messages sent?**

a. $y = \$12.95x + \$0.07$
b. $y = \$13.02x$
c. $y = \frac{\$12.95}{\$0.07}x$
d. $y = \$0.07x + \$12.95$

17. **Hannah draws two supplementary angles. One angle measures 34°. What is the measure of the other angle?**

a. 56°
b. 66°
c. 146°
d. 326°

18. **Part A: Steven's class had a pushup contest and the results are recorded below.**

**What is the median number of pushups the class did?**

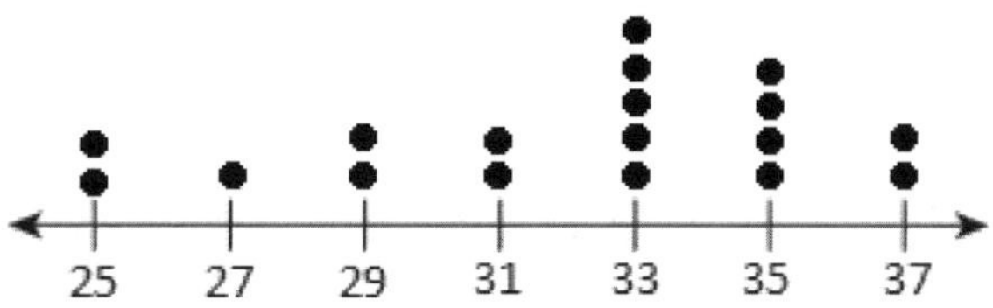


____________________________

**Part B: What is the difference between the median and the mean number of pushups?**

____________________________

19. **A triangle has the following angle measures: 98°, 47°, and 35°. What type of triangle is it?**

a. Obtuse
b. Right
c. Acute
d. Equiangular

20. **Part A: Jordan has a bag full of red and blue marbles. There are 16 red marbles and 24 blue marbles? What is the probability of him drawing a red marble?**

____________________________

**Part B: Jordan has continued to draw marbles and has now taken out 4 red and 6 blue. What is the probability of him drawing a red marble now?**

____________________________

21. **Which figure has two circular bases and a lateral face?**

a. Cone
b. Prism
c. Cylinder
d. Sphere

22. Plot the two ordered pairs on the graph below: (x-3, 5) and (7-x, -2) where x = 2.

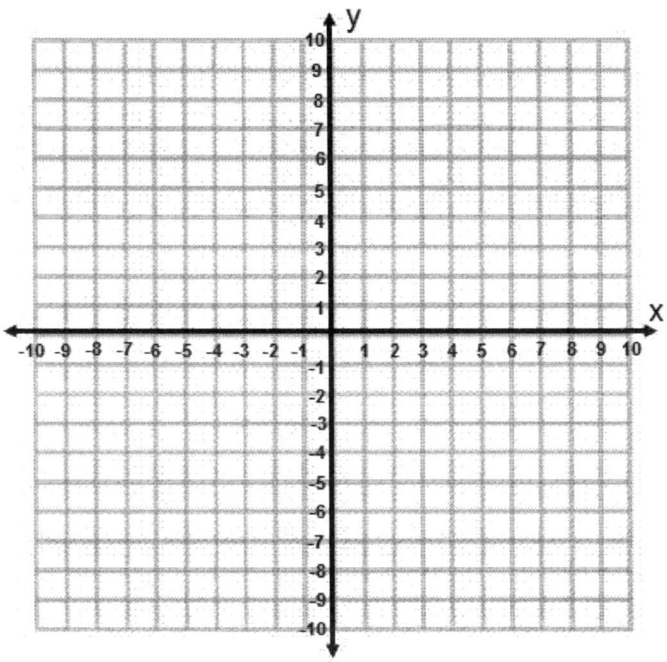


23. Bookstore A sells a particular book for $15.25, but they have it on sale for 20% off. Bookstore B sells it for $12.45. How much more does it cost at Bookstore B?

______________________________

24. A carpenter must fix a broken section of a kitchen cabinet. The intact portion of the cabinet forms a 76 degree angle with the wall. The width of the cabinet is supposed to form a 90 degree angle with the wall. What angle measure should the carpenter use when cutting the piece that will fit next to the 76 degree angle?

a. 12°
b. 14°
c. 104°
d. 136°

**25. Which of the following represents the net of a triangular prism?**

a.

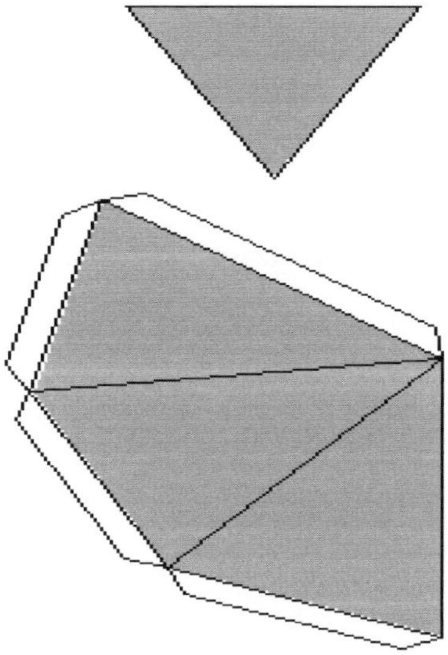

c.

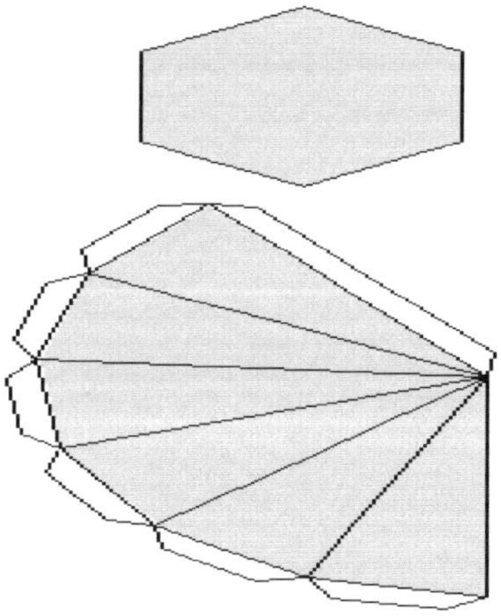

b.

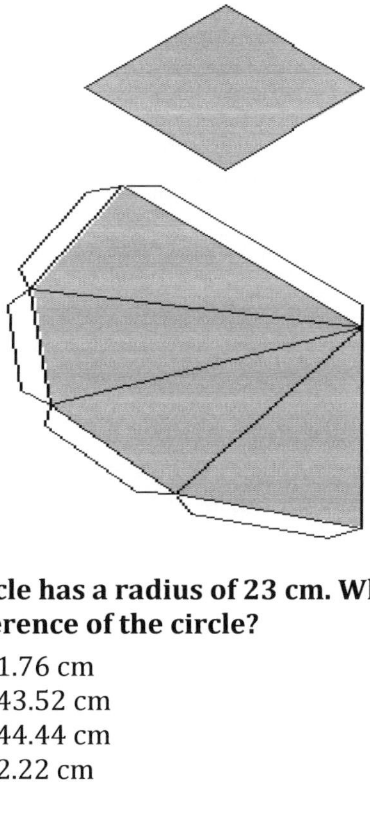

d.

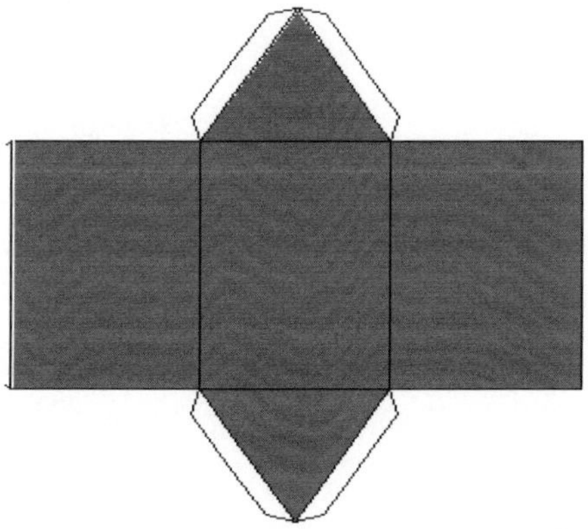

**26. A circle has a radius of 23 cm. Which of the following is the best estimate for the circumference of the circle?**

a. 71.76 cm
b. 143.52 cm
c. 144.44 cm
d. 72.22 cm

**27. Sally is driving to the store. It takes her $\frac{1}{12}$ of an hour to go 3.4 miles. How many miles an hour is Sally driving?**

a. 36 mph
b. 17 mph
c. 40.8 mph
d. 42.4 mph

**28. Which of the following is also equal to $4n^2 + (3n+5)^2$? Select all that apply.**

1. $2n^2 + 2n^2 + (3n+5)^2$
2. $4n^2 + (3n^2 + 25)$
3. $4n^2 + (3n + 5)$
4. $13n^2 + 30n + 25$
5. $7n^2 + 25$

**29. Ashton draws the parallelogram shown below. How many square units represent the area of the parallelogram?**

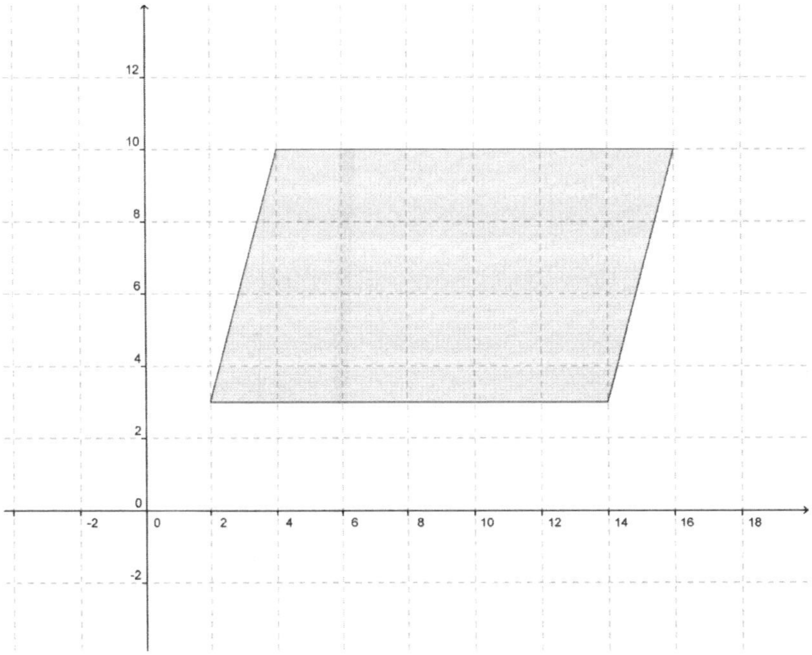


______________________________

**30. In the formula for the volume of the figure shown below, written as $V = B \cdot h$, $h$ represents the height of the prism when it rests one of its bases. What does the $B$ represent?**

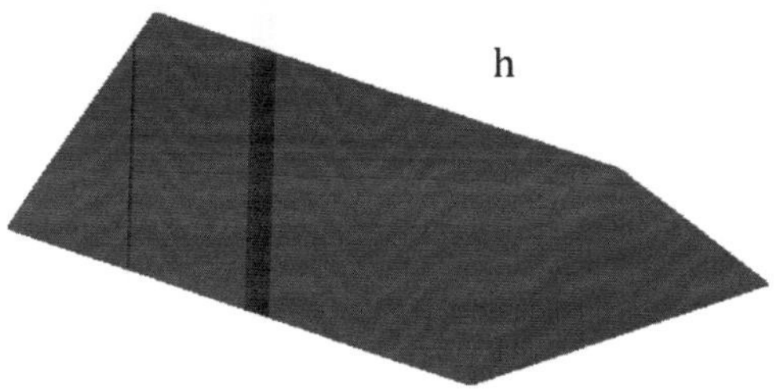


a. $\frac{1}{3}bh$, where b represents the length of the triangle's base and h represents the triangle's height
b. $bh$, where b represents the length of the triangle's base and h represents the triangle's height
c. $2bh$,where b represents the length of triangle's base and h represents the triangle's height
d. $\frac{1}{2}bh$, where b represents the length of triangle's base and h represents the triangle's height

**31. A rectangular prism has a length of 14.3 cm, a width of 8.9 cm, and a height of 11.7 cm. Which of the following is the best estimate for the volume of the rectangular prism?**

a. 1,512 $cm^3$
b. 1,287 $cm^3$
c. 1,386 $cm^3$
d. 1,620 $cm^3$

**32. A can has a radius of 3.5 cm and a height of 8 cm. Which of the following best represents the volume of the can?**

a. 294.86 $cm^3$
b. 298.48 $cm^3$
c. 307.72 $cm^3$
d. 309.24 $cm^3$

**33. Fred designs a candy box in the shape of a triangular prism. The base of each triangular face measures 4 inches, while the height of the prism is 7 inches. Given that the length of the prism is 11 inches, what is the volume of the candy box?**

a. 102 $in^3$
b. 128 $in^3$
c. 154 $in^3$
d. 308 $in^3$

**34. Miranda rolls a standard die and spins a spinner with 4 equal sections. Which of the following represents the sample space?**

a. 10
b. 12
c. 24
d. 36

**35. A hat contains 6 red dice, 4 green dice, and 2 blue dice. What is the probability that Sarah pulls out a blue die, replaces it, and then pulls out a green die?**

a. $\frac{1}{18}$
b. $\frac{1}{3}$
c. $\frac{1}{2}$
d. $\frac{1}{16}$

**36. The histogram below represents the overall GRE scores for a sample of college students. Which of the following is a true statement?**

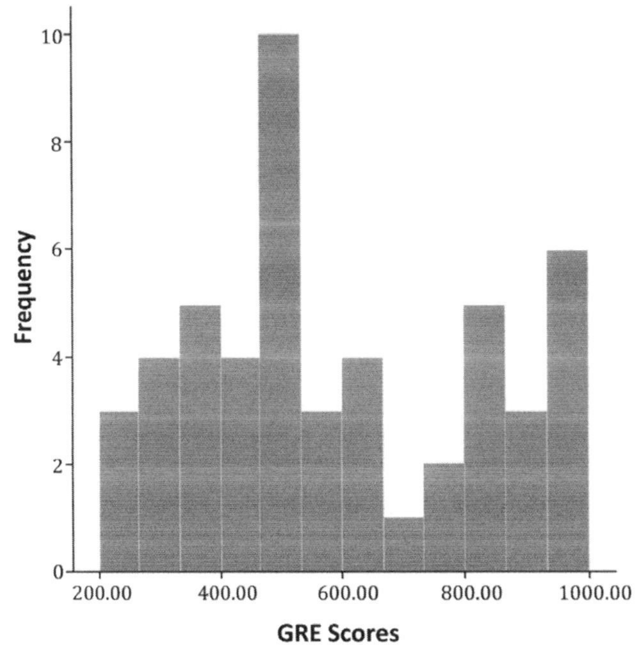


a. The range of GRE scores is approximately 600.
b. The average GRE score is 750.
c. The median GRE score is approximately 500.
d. The fewest number of college students had an approximate score of 800.

**37. What is the area of the circle on the graph below? Each square represents 1 inch.**

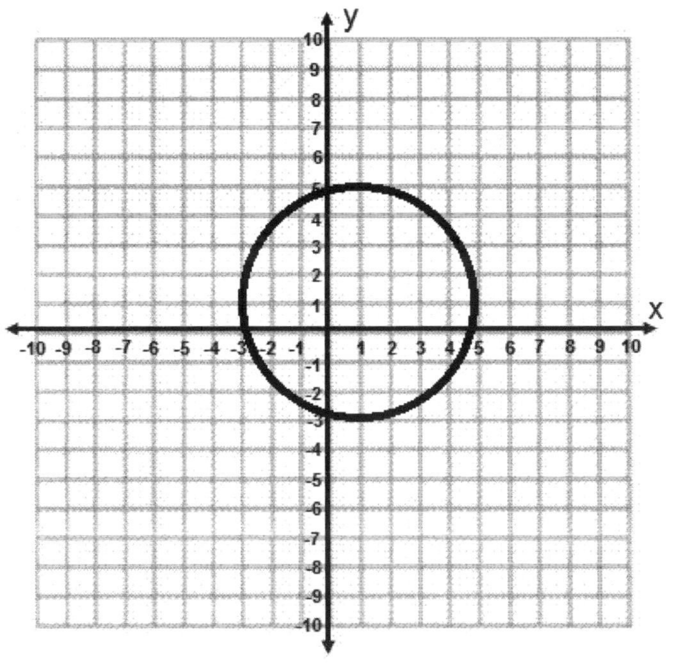

38. **Raymond has the triangular prism shown below. If he cuts two-dimensional slices out of it how many different shapes could he make?**

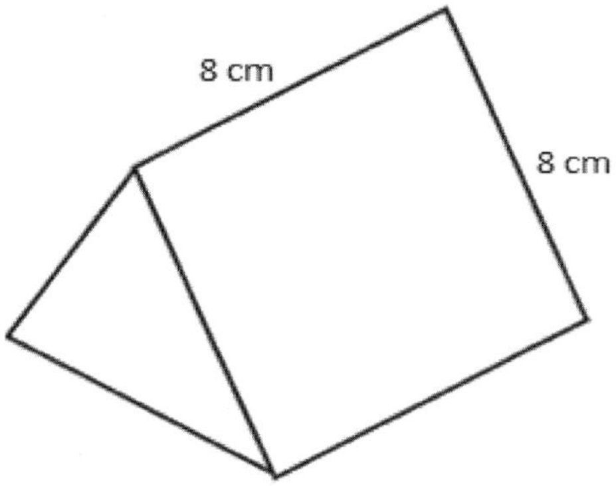


a. 2, a triangle and a rectangle
b. 1, a triangle
c. 2, a square and a rectangle
d. 3, a square, a triangle, and a rectangle`

39. **Gabriel went to a taco shop for lunch. He ordered 3 tacos and paid $4.14. The next day he decided to try a different taco shop and ordered 4 tacos and paid $4.80. How much more expensive was the first taco shop per taco? Express your answer as a percent.**

_______________

40. **Amy rolled a die and flipped a coin and spun a spinner with four equal sections numbered 1-4. What is the probability that she rolled an even number, got heads and then spun an even number?**

a. $\frac{1}{4}$
b. $\frac{1}{2}$
c. $\frac{3}{4}$
d. $\frac{1}{8}$

# Answers and Explanations

**1. D:** In order to convert the given fraction to a percentage, divide 2 by 7. Doing so gives a decimal of approximately 0.29. The decimal can be converted to a percentage by multiplying by 100, which moves the decimal point two places to the right and gives 29%.

**2.** $2n + (3n - 2)^2 = 2n + 9n^2 - 6n - 6n + 4 = 9n^2 - 10n + 4$

**3. D:** In order to determine the amount available to each guest, the total amount of prepared lemonade should be divided by 25 guests. Thus, the expression $2\frac{1}{2} \div 25$ represents the amount that each guest has available for consumption. The mixed fraction can be rewritten as $\frac{5}{2}$. The expression can be simplified by writing $\frac{5}{2} \div 25 = \frac{5}{2} \times \frac{1}{25}$, which equals $\frac{5}{50}$, or $\frac{1}{10}$.

**4.** M=$\frac{1}{2}$, N=1$\frac{3}{4}$, and O=2$\frac{1}{4}$, so N-M+O=3$\frac{1}{2}$. The number line is shown below.

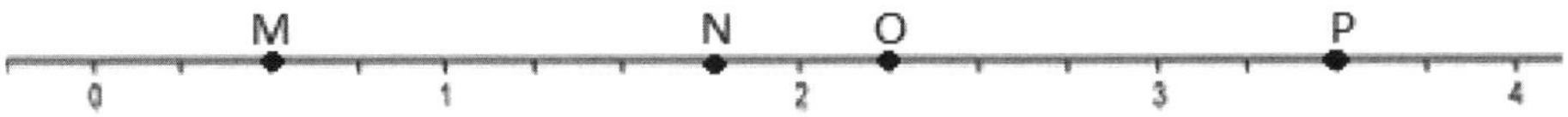


**5. Part A: 44:** I the spinner must land on a different number each time then the highest three numbers are 12,14, and 18. Added together they equal 44.

**Part B: $\frac{3}{4}$:** He has already landed on three of the four numbers so the probability is $\frac{3}{4}$.

**6. D:** The cost per ounce can be calculated by dividing the cost of the bag by the number of ounces the bag contains. Thus, the cost per ounce can be calculated by writing $9.85 ÷ 16, which equals approximately $0.62 per ounce.

**7. D:** The order of operations states that numbers with exponents must be evaluated first. Thus, the expression can be rewritten as $64 + 12 \div 4 + 64 \times 3$. Next, multiplication and division must be computed as they appear from left to right in the expression. Thus, the expression can be further simplified as $64 + 3 + 192$, which equals 259.

**8. Part A: C:** Both flour and butter are given in cups so they are easy to compare. First find a like denominator. $\frac{1}{2}$ is equal to $\frac{2}{4}$, and $1\frac{3}{4}$ is equal to $\frac{7}{4}$. So the ratio is 2:7.

**Part B: 3:7, 4:7:** This question is very similar to Part A. Both milk and flour are given in cups and fourths. It's $\frac{3}{4}$ to $\frac{7}{4}$ or 3:7, and if she puts a whole cup in then its $\frac{4}{4}$ to $\frac{7}{4}$ or 4:7.

**9. Part A: B:** The discounted price is 25% less than the original price. Therefore, the discounted price can be written as $36.95 - ((0.25)(36.95))$, which equals approximately 27.71. Thus, the discounted price of the jacket is $27.71.

**Part B: $29.93:** If sales tax is 8% then that can be written as ($27.71)(1.08), which is approximately $29.93.

**10. 1479 miles:** The first day they went 69 miles per hour for 11 hours, so they went $11 \times 69 = 759\ miles$. The second day they went 72 miles per hour for 10 hours, so they went $10 \times 72 = 720\ miles$. Total they went 1479 miles.

**11. B:** In order to find the unit rate, the cost of the bottle should be divided by the number of fluid ounces contained in the bottle: $\frac{\$3.96}{20} \approx 0.20$. Thus, the cost per fluid ounce is approximately \$0.20.

**12. X=4:** $3^2 + 2x = 17, 9 + 2x = 17, 2x = 8, x = 4$

**13. 47 square inches: The top left shaded region can be found by first finding the width.** Since 6 in. is given as the width of the whole rectangle and 4 in. is given for the width of the non shaded region then the width of the shaded region is the difference of 2 inches. So, the area of that region is $7\ in. \times 2in. = 14\ square\ inches$. The other shaded region can be broken into a 3 in. by 3 in. square and a 4 in. by 6 in. rectangle. So, $3\ in. \times 3\ in. = 9\ ssquare\ inches$ and $4\ in. \times 6\ in. = 24\ square\ inches$. Added together, 14 square inches + 9 square inches + 24 square inches = 47 square inches.

**14. C:** The equation that represents the relationship between the position number, *n*, and the value of the term, $a_n$, is $a_n = -3n + 8$. Notice each *n* is multiplied by −3, with 8 added to that value. Substituting position number 1 for *n* gives $a_n = -3(1) + 8$, which equals 5. Substitution of the remaining position numbers does not provide a counterexample to this procedure.

**15. B:** All given sequences have a constant difference of 12. Subtraction of 12 from the starting term, given for Choice B, gives a *y*-intercept of −9. The equation $123 = 12x - 9$ can thus be written. Solving for *x* gives $x = 11$; therefore, 123 is indeed the $11^{th}$ term of this sequence. Manual computation of the $11^{th}$ term by adding the constant difference of 12 also reveals 123 as the value of the $11^{th}$ term of this sequence.

**16. D:** The constant amount Kevin pays is \$12.95; this amount represents the *y*-intercept. The variable amount is represented by the expression $\$0.07x$, where *x* represents the number of text messages sent and \$0.07 represents the constant rate of change or slope. Thus, his total cost can be represented by the equation $y = \$0.07x + \$12.95$.

**17. C:** Supplementary angles add to 180 degrees. Therefore, the other angle is equal to the difference between 180 degrees and 34 degrees: $180 - 34 = 146$. Thus, the other angle measures 146°.

**18. Part A: 33:** The median number is the middle number out of the group. In this case there are 18 numbers so it is the average of the $9^{th}$ and $10^{th}$ number. However, since the $9^{th}$ and $10^{th}$ numbers are both 33 it is just 33.

**Part B: 1:** The mean can be found by adding all of the numbers together and dividing by 18. If you add all of the numbers up and divide by 18 you get 32. The difference in the mean and median is 1.

**19. A:** A triangle with an obtuse angle (an angle greater than 90°) is called an obtuse triangle.

**20. Part A: $\frac{2}{5}$:** There are a total of 40 marbles in the bag. The probability of him drawing a red one is $\frac{16}{40}$ or $\frac{2}{5}$.

**Part B: $\frac{2}{3}$:** If 4 red and 6 blue are missing then there are only 12 red and 18 blue remaining. The probability of drawing a red one then is $\frac{12}{18}$ or $\frac{2}{3}$.

**21. C:** A cylinder has two circular bases and a rectangular lateral face.

**22.** The point (x-3, 5) is (2-3, 5) or (-1, 5). The point (7-x, -2) is (7-2, -2) or (5, -2). Both are graphed below.

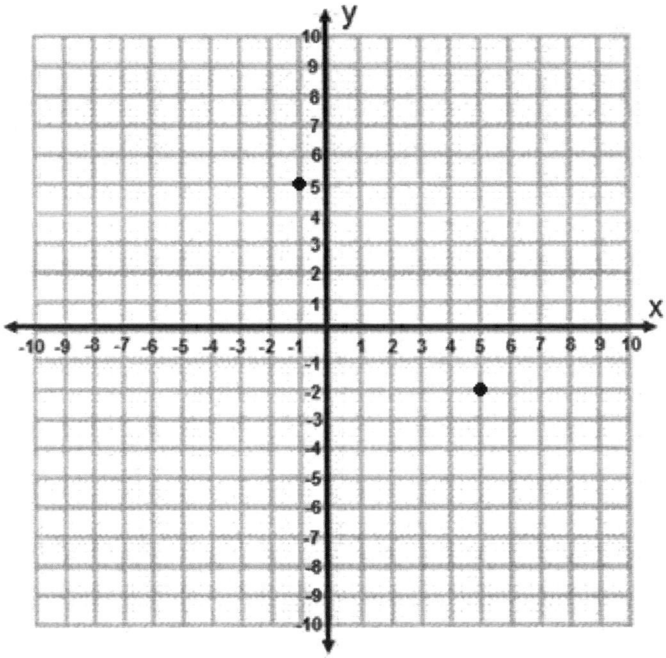

**23. $.25**: First find the cost of the book at Bookstore A. The price would be $\$15.25(.8) = \$12.20$. The cost at Bookstore B is $12.45 so it is $.25 more.

**24. B:** Since the intact portion of the cabinet and the missing piece form a 90 degree angle with the wall, the missing piece must have an angle equal to the difference between 90 degrees and 76 degrees. Thus, the newly cut cabinet piece should have an angle measure of 14 degrees.

**25. D:** A triangular prism has two triangular bases and three rectangular faces.

**26. C:** The circumference of a circle can be determined by using the formula $C = \pi d$. A radius of 23 cm indicates a diameter of 46 cm, or twice that length. Substitution of 46 cm for $d$ and 3.14 for $\pi$ gives the following: $C = 3.14 \cdot 46$, which equals 144.44. Thus, the circumference of the circle is approximately 144.44 cm.

**27. C:** If she goes 3.4 miles in $\frac{1}{12}$ of an hour then just multiply by 12 to see how far she will go in one hour. Then that is her miles per hour.

**28. I, IV:** Start by simplifying the equation. $4n^2 + (3n + 5)^2 = 4n^2 + 9n^2 + 15n + 15n + 25 = 13n^2 + 30n + 25$. So, you can see that you came up with answer IV right there, and answer I is the same as the original equation except for the $4n^2$ is broken down to $2n^2 + 2n^2$.

**29. 84:** The area of a parallelogram can be found by using the formula $A = bh$, where $b$ represents the length of the base and $h$ represents the height of the parallelogram. The base and the height of the parallelogram are 12 units and 7 units, respectively. Therefore, the area can be written as $A = 12 \cdot 7$, which equals 84.

**30. D:** The $B$ in the formula $V = Bh$ represents the area of the triangular base. The formula for the area of a triangle is $\frac{1}{2}bh$, where $b$ represents the length of the triangle's base and $h$ represents the triangle's height.

**31. A:** The dimensions of the rectangular prism can be rounded to 14 cm, 9 cm, and 12 cm. The volume of a rectangular prism can be determined by finding the product of the length, width, and height. Therefore, the volume is approximately equal to $14 \times 9 \times 12$, or 1,512 cm$^3$.

**32. C:** The volume of a cylindrical can be found using the formula $V = \pi r^2 h$, where $r$ represents the radius and $h$ represents the height. Substitution of the given radius and height gives $V = \pi(3.5)^2 \cdot 8$, which is approximately 307.72. Thus, the volume of the can is approximately 307.72 cm$^3$.

**33. C:** The volume of a triangular prism can be determined using the formula $V = \frac{1}{2}bhl$, where $b$ represents the length of the base of each triangular face, $h$ represents the height of each triangular face, and $l$ represents the length of the prism. Substitution of the given values into the formula gives $V = \frac{1}{2} \cdot 4 \cdot 7 \cdot 11$, which equals 154. Thus, the volume of the candy box is 154 cubic inches.

**34. C:** The sample space of independent events is equal to the product of the sample space of each event. The sample space of rolling a die is 6; the sample space of spinning a spinner with four equal sections is 4. Therefore, the overall sample space is equal to 6 × 4, or 24.

**35. A:** The events are independent since Sarah replaces the first die. The probability of two independent events can be found using the formula $P(A\ and\ B) = P(A) \cdot P(B)$. The probability of pulling out a blue die is $\frac{2}{12}$. The probability of pulling out a green die is $\frac{4}{12}$. The probability of pulling out a blue die and a green die is $\frac{2}{12} \cdot \frac{4}{12}$, which simplifies to $\frac{1}{18}$.

**36. C:** The median is the value that splits the data in half. Thus, approximately 50% of the scores are above it and 50% are below it. From the histogram, there are a total of 50 data points, so the median would be located between the 25th and 26th scores when the data are ordered from least to greatest. Counting the frequencies from left to right, the halfway point lies in the interval around 500. Therefore, the median GRE score is approximately 500.

**37. 16π or 50.27 inches:** The area of a circle is $\pi r^2$. You can find the radius by counting the number of units across the circle and dividing by 2. So the radius is 4 inches. $\pi 4^2 = 16\pi\ or\ 50.27\ inches$.

**38. D:** If you were to cut a slice vertically it would produce a triangle. If you were to cut a slice long ways it would produce a rectangle, and if you were to cut a slice that was the front face of the prism it would be an 8 by 8 square.

**39. 15%:** First find the cost of the first taco shop by dividing $4.14 by 3, which comes out to $1.38 per taco. Then find the price at the second shop by dividing $4.80 by 4 to get $1.20 per taco. The difference is .$18. To get a percentage divide $.18 by $1.20 and multiply by 100. The first shop cost 15% more than the second.

**40. D:** The probability of getting an even number is $\frac{3}{6}$. The probability of getting heads is $\frac{1}{2}$. The probability of spinning an even number is $\frac{2}{4}$. The probability of all three occurring can be calculated by multiplying the probabilities of the individual events: $\frac{3}{6} \cdot \frac{1}{2} \cdot \frac{2}{4}$ equals $\frac{1}{8}$.

# Mathematics Practice Test #2

## Practice Questions

**1. Which of the following is the largest number?**

$$\frac{14}{4}, 3.41, \pi, 3\frac{3}{8}$$

______________________________

**2. A plane takes off from Dallas and lands in New York 3 hours and 20 minutes later. The distance from Dallas to New York is 1510 miles. Approximately how fast was the plane traveling?**

a. 445 mph
b. 453 mph
c. 456 mph
d. 449 mph

**3. According to the order of operations, which of the following steps should be completed immediately following the evaluation of the squared number when evaluating the expression $9 - 18^2 \times 2 + 12 \div 4$?**

a. Subtract $18^2$ from 9
b. Multiply the squared value by 2
c. Divide 12 by 4
d. Add 2 and 12

**4. A parcel of land has 35 mature trees for every 3 acres. How many mature trees can be found on 18 of the acres?**

a. 206
b. 212
c. 210
d. 214

**5. Which of the following is equivalent to $-8^2 + (17 - 9) \times 4 + 7$?**

a. −217
b. 24
c. −64
d. −25

**6. Jason chooses a number that is the square root of four less than two times Amy's number. If Amy's number is 20, what is Jason's number?**

a. 6
b. 7
c. 8
d. 9

**7. Part A: What is the area of the shaded region below?**

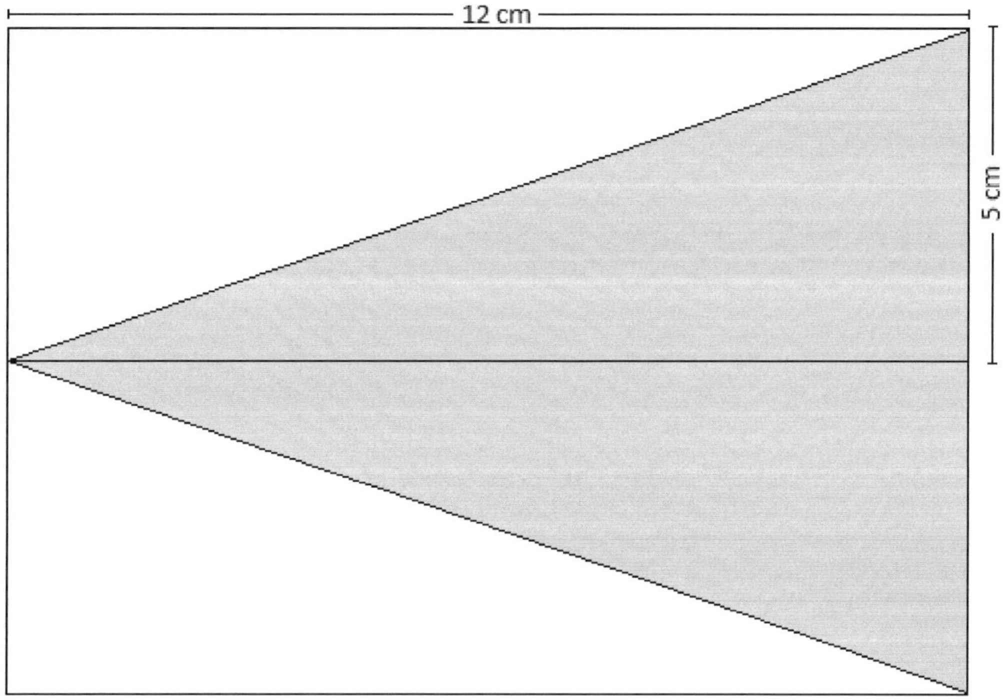


____________________________________

**Part B: How does the shaded region compare to the non shaded region?**

a. The shaded region is bigger than the non shaded region
b. Both the shaded and non shaded region are the same size
c. The non shaded region is bigger than the shaded region
d. The area of the non shaded region cannot be determined

**8. Given the table below what would *y* be if *x=5*?**

| x | -2 | 0 | 3 | 4 |
|---|---|---|---|---|
| y | 2 | -2 | 7 | 14 |

a. 21
b. 23
c. 19
d. 24

**9. Given the following equation what is *x* equal to if *y* equals 8? $6x + 4 = 2y - 7$.**

____________________________________

**10. A landscaping company charges \$25 per $\frac{1}{2}$-acre to mow a yard. The company is offering a 20% discount for the month of May. If Douglas has a two-acre yard, how much will the company charge?**

a. \$65
b. \$80
c. \$70
d. \$75

**11. A house is priced at \$278,000. The price of the house has been reduced by \$12,600. Which of the following best represents the percentage of the reduction?**

a. 3%
b. 4%
c. 5%
d. 6%

**12. Amy buys 4 apples and 3 bananas at the grocery store. She spent a total of \$5.17. Each apple cost \$.94. If each banana cost the same amount how much did one banana cost?**

______________________________

**13. Melanie makes \$12 an hour and is taxed at 15% on her income. Lynn makes \$14 an hour and is taxed at 18% on her income. If they both work a 40 hour week, how much more does Lynn make than Melanie?**

______________________________

**14. A cone has a radius of 4 cm and an approximate volume of 150.72 $cm^3$. What is the height of the cone?**

a. 7 cm
b. 9 cm
c. 8 cm
d. 12 cm

**15. What is the range of the points on the number line below?**

______________________________

**16. Complete the equation below.**

$2\frac{5}{8}-\frac{3}{2}+\left(\frac{2}{3}-\frac{1}{6}\right)=1\frac{1}{8}+$__________=__________

**17. Point S and Point T are shown on the number line below. Which of the following equations produces a point, *R*, not on the number line?**

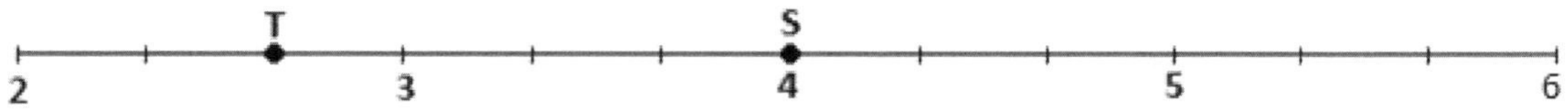


a. 2S-T=R
b. 2T-S=R
c. 3T-S=R
d. 3S-2T=R

**18. Part A: The spinner below is spun once. What is the probability of landing on a 12 or greater?**

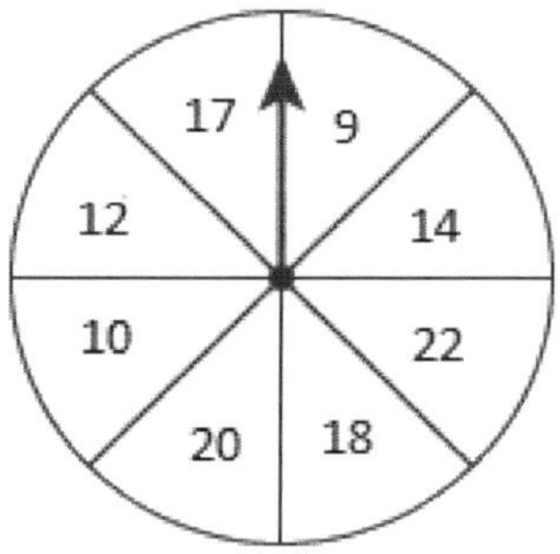


a. $\frac{5}{8}$
b. $\frac{1}{2}$
c. $\frac{3}{4}$
d. $\frac{2}{8}$

**Part B: What is the probability of spinning it a second time and getting a 12 or greater both times?**

____________________________

**19. A toy store owner sells action figures. He buys each one from the manufacture for $4.10. He has labor and other costs of $1.35 per action figure. He wants to make a 32% profit on each one. How much does he need to sell them for?**

____________________________

**20. Angle A and Angle B are complementary. Angle B measures 28°. What is the measure of Angle A?**

a. 62°
b. 92°
c. 72°
d. 152°

**21. Which of the following describes *all* requirements of similar polygons?**

a. Similar polygons have congruent corresponding angles and proportional corresponding sides
b. Similar polygons have congruent corresponding angles and congruent corresponding sides
c. Similar polygons have proportional corresponding sides
d. Similar polygons have congruent corresponding angles

**22. How far apart are the two points on the graph below? Each square represents 3 feet.**

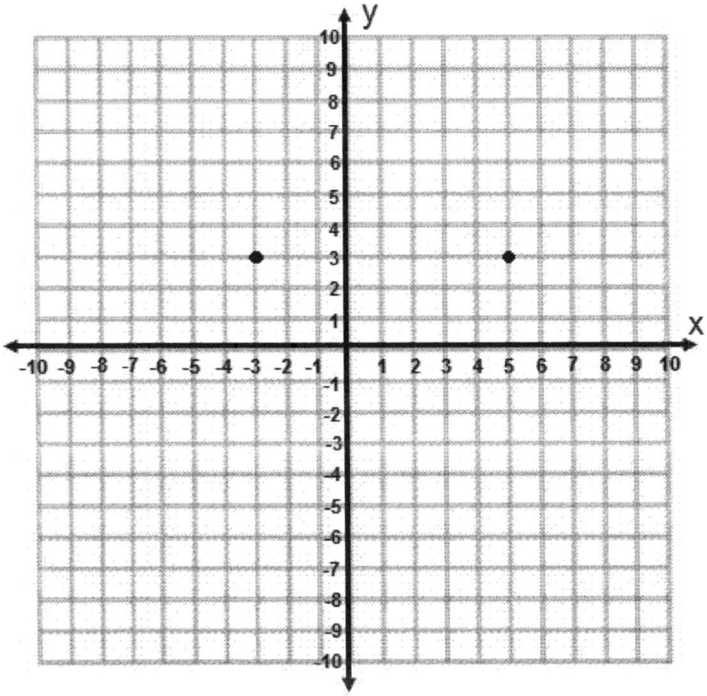


a. 15 feet
b. 22 feet
c. 21 feet
d. 24 feet

**23. Eric is able to dribble the soccer ball down $\frac{2}{3}$ of the field in $\frac{2}{5}$ of a minute. How long will it take him to dribble the whole field?**

a. 36 seconds
b. 24 seconds
c. 30 seconds
d. 32 seconds

**24. Kaleb has a bike rim that is 18 inches in diameter. He puts a tire on it that is 2 inches thick. What is the circumference of the tire?**

a. $20\pi$
b. $22\pi$
c. $24\pi$
d. $18\pi$

**25. Given the trapezoid shown below, which of the following vertices represent the reflection of the trapezoid across the $y$-axis?**

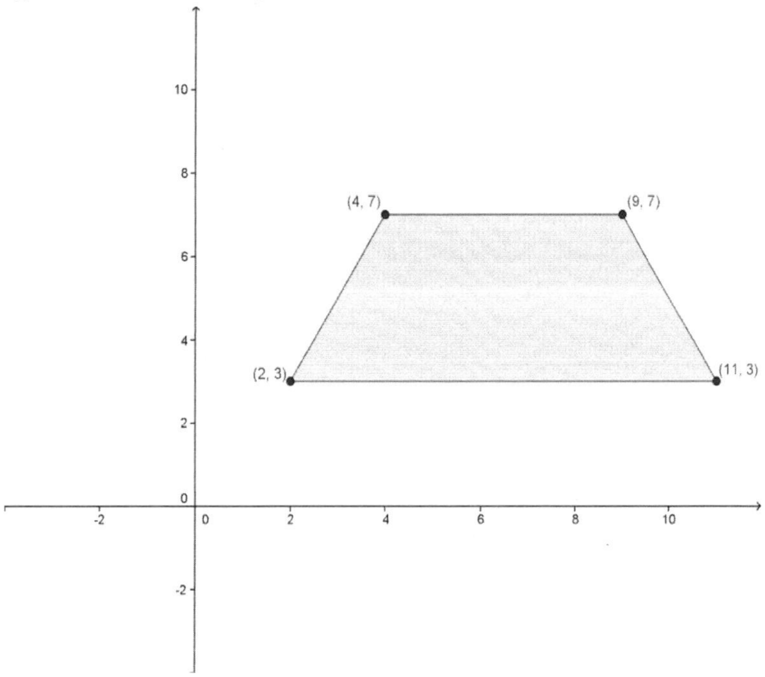


a. $(-4,-7), (-9,-7), (-2,-3), (-11,-3)$
b. $(-4,7), (-9,7), (-2,3), (-11,3)$
c. $(7,-4), (7,-9), (3,-2), (3,-11)$
d. $(4,-7), (9,-7), (2,-3), (11,-3)$

**26. A regular heptagon has each side length equal to 9.2 cm. Which of the following is the best estimate for the perimeter of the heptagon?**

a. 60 cm
b. 63 cm
c. 54 cm
d. 70 cm

**27. A parallelogram has two bases, each equal to 18 cm, and a height of 8 cm. What is the area of the parallelogram?**

a. 288 $cm^2$
b. 72 $cm^2$
c. 144 $cm^2$
d. 96 $cm^2$

**28. Which of the following represents the area of the triangle shown below?**

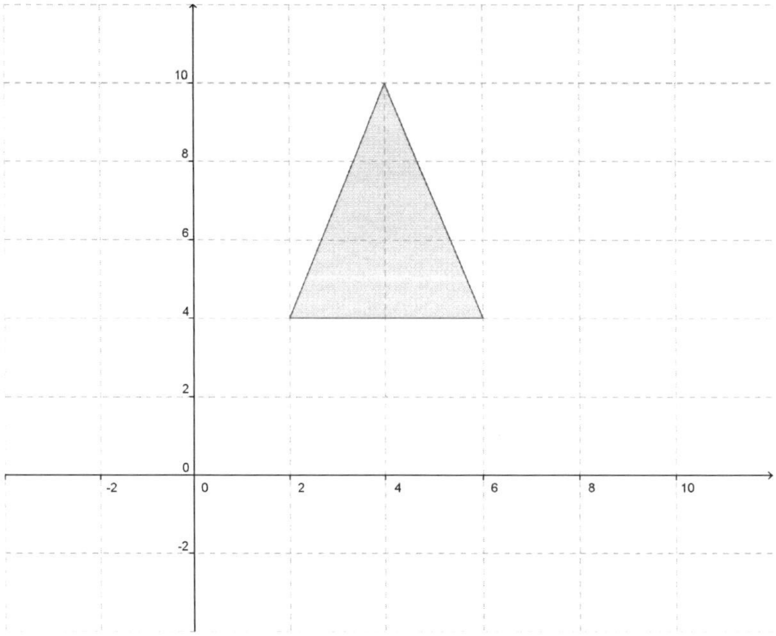


a. 8 square units
b. 9 square units
c. 10 square units
d. 12 square units

**29. Judith purchased a box from the U.S. Postal Service with dimensions of 12 inches by 8 inches by 6 inches. How many cubic inches of space inside the box does she have available for use?**

________________________________

**30. A pothole has a radius of 9 inches. Which of the following best represents the distance around the pothole?**

a. 14.13 inches
b. 28.26 inches
c. 42.39 inches
d. 56.52 inches

**31. What is the area of a trapezoid with base lengths of 7 cm and 10 cm and a height of 5 cm?**

a. 85 $cm^2$
b. 42.5 $cm^2$
c. 28 $cm^2$
d. 8.5 $cm^2$

**32. What is the sample space when rolling two standard dice?**

a. 18
b. 6
c. 12
d. 36

**33. What is the sample space when flipping a coin 9 times?**

a. 256
b. 4,096
c. 512
d. 1,028

**34. Kevin spins a spinner with 8 sections labeled 1 through 8. He also flips a coin. What is the probability he will land on a number less than 5 and get tails?**

a. $\frac{7}{8}$
b. $\frac{1}{4}$
c. $\frac{5}{16}$
d. $\frac{1}{2}$

**35. A box contains 8 yellow marbles, 9 orange marbles, and 1 green marble. What is the probability that Ann pulls out a yellow marble, replaces it, and then pulls a green marble?**

a. $\frac{4}{153}$
b. $\frac{1}{2}$
c. $\frac{4}{9}$
d. $\frac{2}{81}$

**36. The number of flights a flight attendant made per month is represented by the line graph below.**

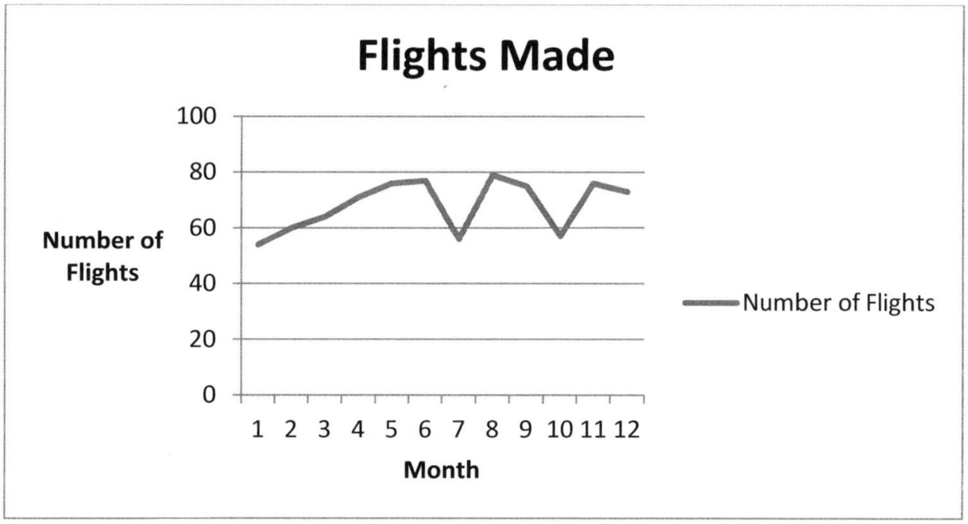


**What is the range in the number of flights the flight attendant made?**

a. 20
b. 25
c. 29
d. 32

**37. Aubrey planted fruit trees on her farm. The number of each type of tree planted is shown in the table below.**

| Type of Tree | Number of Trees |
|---|---|
| Apple Tree | 8 |
| Peach Tree | 18 |
| Fig Tree | 12 |
| Pear Tree | 3 |

**Which circle graph represents the percentage of each type of tree planted?**

a.
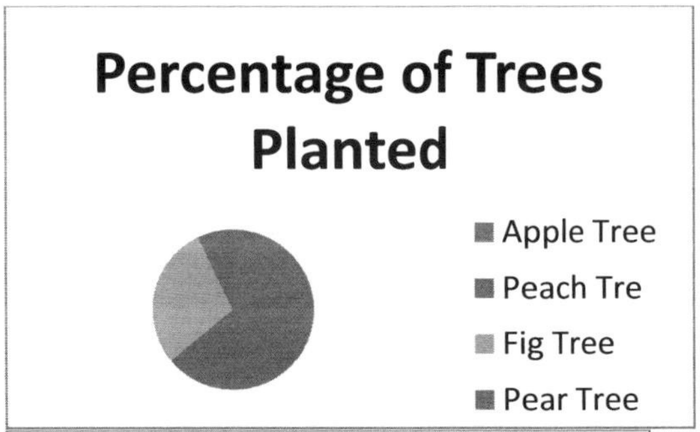


b.
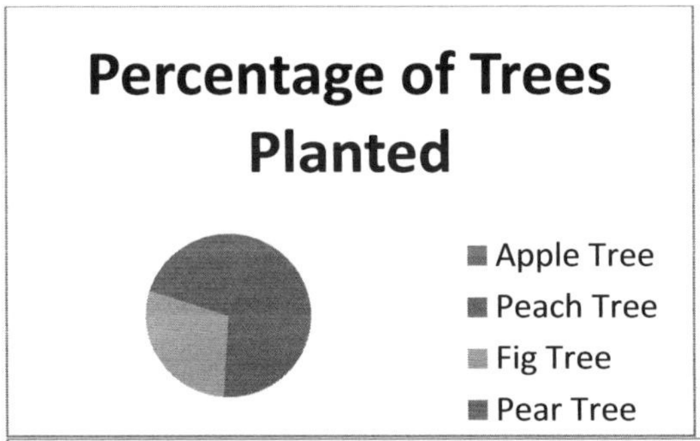


c.
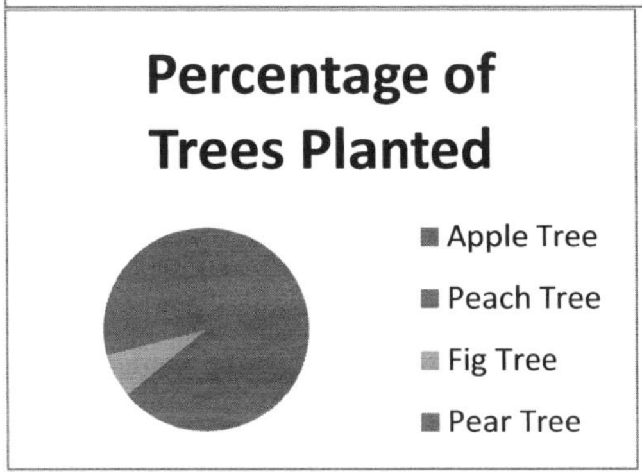


d.
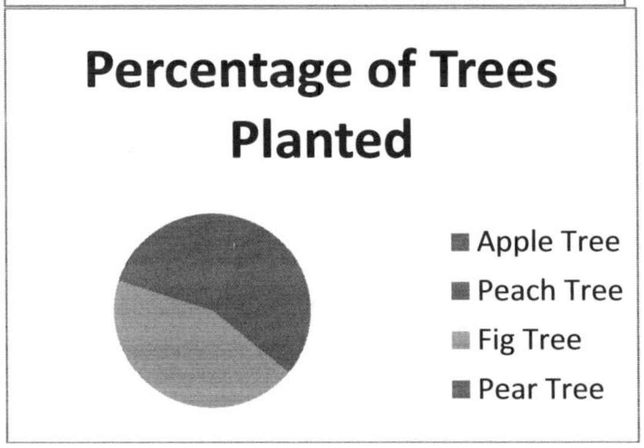


**38. Chandler wishes to examine the median house value in his new hometown. Which graphical representation will most clearly indicate the median?**

a. Box-and-whisker plot
b. Stem-and-leaf plot
c. Line plot
d. Bar graph

**39. Part A: The number of long distance minutes Amanda used per week for business purposes is shown in the table below.**

| Week | Number of Minutes |
|---|---|
| 1 | 289 |
| 2 | 255 |
| 3 | 322 |
| 4 | 291 |
| 5 | 306 |
| 6 | 302 |
| 7 | 411 |
| 8 | 418 |

**What is the median number of long distance minutes she used?**

______________________

**Part B: How much more is the mean than the median?**

______________________

**40. A university reported the number of incoming freshmen from 2002 to 2011. The data is shown in the table below.**

| Year | Number of Incoming Freshmen |
|---|---|
| 2002 | 7,046 |
| 2003 | 7,412 |
| 2004 | 6,938 |
| 2005 | 7,017 |
| 2006 | 7,692 |
| 2007 | 8,784 |
| 2008 | 7,929 |
| 2009 | 7,086 |
| 2010 | 8,017 |
| 2011 | 8,225 |

**Based on the 10-year sample of data, which of the following represents the approximate average number of incoming freshmen?**

a. 7,618
b. 7,615
c. 7,621
d. 7,624

## Answers and Explanations

**1. $\frac{14}{4}$:** First you will want to convert all of the numbers to a decimal so they will be easier to compare. $\frac{14}{4} = 3.5, 3.41, \pi = 3.14, 3\frac{3}{8} = 3.375$. Once they are all in decimal form you can see that 3.5 or $\frac{14}{4}$ is the biggest.

**2. B:** To find miles per hour just divide the number of miles by the number of hours. In this case 3 hours and 20 minutes is equal to $3\frac{1}{3}$ hours. 1510 divided by $3\frac{1}{3}$ is approximately 453 mph.

**3. B:** The order of operations states that multiplication and division, as they appear from left to right in the expression, should be completed following the evaluation of exponents. Therefore, after evaluating the squared number, that value should be multiplied by 2.

**4. C:** The following proportion can be used to solve the problem: $\frac{35}{3} = \frac{x}{18}$, where *x* represents the number of mature trees. Solving for *x* gives $3x = 630$, which simplifies to $x = 210$.

**5. D:** The order of operations requires evaluation of the expression inside the parentheses as a first step. Thus, the expression can be re-written as $-8^2 + 8 \times 4 + 7$ . Next, the integer with the exponent must be evaluated. Doing so gives $-64 + 8 \times 4 + 7$. The order of operations next requires all multiplications and divisions to be computed as they appear from left to right. Thus, the expression can be written as $-64 + 32 + 7$. Finally, the addition may be computed as it appears from left to right. The expression simplifies to $-32 + 7$, or −25.

**6. A:** Jason's number can be determined by writing the following expression: $\sqrt{2x - 4}$, where *x* represents Amy's number. Substitution of 20 for *x* gives $\sqrt{2(20) - 4}$, which simplifies to $\sqrt{36}$, or 6. Thus, Jason's number is 6. Jason's number can also be determined by working backwards. If Jason's number is the square root of 4 less than 2 times Amy's number, Amy's number should first be multiplied by 2 with 4 subtracted from that product and the square root taken of the resulting difference.

**7. Part A:** Since the line that divides the shaded and non shaded region runs from corner to corner it cuts the rectangle in half. This means you can just find the area of the rectangle and divide by 2. However there are two smaller rectangles like this. So, if you take half of each that is the same as one whole rectangle. The area of the rectangle is 5 cm times 12 cm which is 60 cm. Since you would divide by 2 to get the area of one but then multiply back by 2 to get the area of both there is no need to do either. The area of the shaded region is 60 sq cm.

**Part B: B:** As mentioned in Part A, since the line that divides them cuts the rectangle in half they are the same size.

**8. 23:** First find the relationship between *x* and *y*. When *x*=0 then *y*=-2, so this means that the equation is will have a -2 in it. If you add 2 back to all of the *y* numbers then you can see that they are the squares of the *x's*. So the relationship is $y = x^2 - 2$. Then you can just plug in to find the when *x*=5, *y*=23.

**9.$\frac{5}{6}$:** First plug 8 in for *y* to get $6x + 4 = 2(8) - 7$. Then solve for *x*. $6x + 4 = 16 - 7, 6x = 5, x = \frac{5}{6}$.

**10. B:** Based on the company's charge per half of an acre, the original charge is equal to $25 × 4, or $100, since there are 4 half-acres in 2 acres. With the discount of 20%, the following expression can be used to determine the final charge: $x - 0.20x$, where $x$ represents the original charge. Substitution of 100 for $x$ gives $100 - 0.20(100)$, which equals $100 - 20$, or 80. Thus, the company will charge \$80.

**11. B:** The original price was \$290,600 (\$278,000 + \$12,600). In order to determine the percentage of reduction, the following equation can be written: $\$12{,}600 = \$290{,}600x$, which simplifies to $x \approx 0.04$ , or 4%. Thus, the percentage of reduction was approximately 4%.

**12. \$.47:** The total was \$5.17 and the 4 apples cost \$3.76. So, \$5.17-\$3.76=\$1.41 that was spent on bananas. Since there were 3 bananas, divide \$1.41 by 3 to get \$.47 per banana.

**13. \$51.20:** First find what Melanie makes in a week. She makes \$12 an hour times 40 hours, so she makes \$480. Then take off 15% percent for her taxes. \$480(.85)=\$408. Next find what Lynn makes in one week. She makes \$14 an hour times 40 hours, so she makes \$560. Then take 18% off for her taxes. \$560(.82)=\$459.20. Then subtract what Melanie makes from what Lynn makes to find out how much more Lynn makes. \$459.20-\$408= \$51.20.

**14. B:** The volume of a cone can be determined by using the formula $V = \frac{1}{3}\pi r^2 h$. Substitution of the radius and volume into the formula gives $150.72 = \frac{1}{3}\pi(4)^2 h$, which simplifies to $150.72 = \frac{1}{3}\pi 16h$. Division of each side of the equation by $\frac{1}{3}\pi 16$ gives $h = 9$. Thus, the height of the cone is 9 cm.

**15. 3:** The range of the numbers is the difference between the largest and smallest numbers in a set of numbers. In this case each tick mark on the number line represents $\frac{1}{2}$. The smallest number plotted is $5\frac{1}{2}$ and the largest number is $8\frac{1}{2}$. The range is 3.

**16. $\frac{1}{2}$, $1\frac{5}{8}$:** $2\frac{1}{2} - \frac{3}{2}$ is already given as $1\frac{1}{8}$. Inside the parentheses convert the $\frac{2}{3}$ to $\frac{4}{6}$. Then you can do $\frac{4}{6} - \frac{1}{6} = \frac{3}{6} = \frac{1}{2}$. The first space is $\frac{1}{2}$. Then $1\frac{1}{8} + \frac{1}{2} = 1\frac{5}{8}$. The second space is $1\frac{5}{8}$.

**17. B:** Point T is equal to $2\frac{2}{3}$ and S is equal to 4. Perform all of the equations to figure out which one produces a number that is not on the number line. 2T-S= $2(2\frac{2}{3})$-4= $1\frac{1}{3}$ which is not on the number line.

**18. Part A: C:** There are a total of 8 spaces on the spinner all of equal size. There are 6 spaces that are 12 or greater. $\frac{6}{8} = \frac{3}{4}$.

**Part B: $\frac{9}{16}$:** The first time the probability was $\frac{3}{4}$ and the second time the probability is also $\frac{3}{4}$. The probability of it happening both times though is $\frac{3}{4} \times \frac{3}{4}$ which is $\frac{9}{16}$.

**19. \$7.02:** If he buys each toy for \$4.10 and then has another \$1.30 in it, then he has a total of \$5.40 in each toy. He marks it up 30% to sell it so his sales price is \$5.40(1.30)=\$7.02.

**20. A:** Complementary angles sum to 90 degrees. Since Angle B measures 28°, Angle A measures $90° - 28°$, or 62°.

**21. A:** Similar polygons must have congruent corresponding angles and proportional corresponding sides. Both requirements must be fulfilled in order to declare similarity in polygons.

**22. D:** One point is at (-3, 3) and the other is at (5, 3). So, they are at a distance of 8. Since each square is equal to 3 feet they are 24 feet apart.

**23. A:** If it takes him $\frac{2}{5}$ of a minute to dribble $\frac{2}{3}$ of the field then divide by 2 to get $\frac{1}{5}$ of a minute for $\frac{1}{3}$ of the field. Then you can multiply by 3 to get $\frac{3}{3}$ of the field in $\frac{3}{5}$ of a minute. $\frac{3}{5}$ of a minute equals 36 seconds.

**24. C:** If he puts a tire on that is 2 inches thick then that adds 4 inches to the overall diameter. Now the radius is 12 inches. The formula for circumference is $2\pi r$. 2 times $12\pi$ is $24\pi$.

**25. B:** A reflection of a figure across the $y$-axis is achieved by finding the additive inverse of each $x$-value. The $y$-values will not change. Therefore, the vertices of the reflected figure are (−4, 7), (−9, 7), (−2, 3), and (−11, 3).

**26. B:** A regular heptagon has equal side lengths. Thus, an estimate for the perimeter can be computed by rounding the given side length and multiplying by 7 (the number of sides of a heptagon); 9.2 can be rounded to 9, and 9 × 7 =63. Thus, the best estimate for the perimeter of the heptagon is 63 cm.

**27. C:** The area of a parallelogram can be calculated using the formula $A = bh$. The length of the base of the parallelogram is 18 cm, and the height is 8 cm. Thus, the area is equal to 18 × 8 $cm^2$, or 144 $cm^2$.

**28. D:** The given triangle has a base equal to 4 units and a height equal to 6 units. Thus, the area of the triangle is equal to $\frac{1}{2}(4)(6)$ square units, or 12 square units.

**29.** The correct answer is **576.** The box is a rectangular prism, and the amount of available space inside the box is synonymous with the volume of the box. The volume of a rectangular prism is calculated by finding the product of the length, width, and height. Thus, the volume of the box is equal to 12 in × 8 in × 6 in, or 576 cubic inches.

**30. D:** The distance around the pothole indicates the circumference of the pothole. The circumference of a circle can be determined by using the formula $C = \pi d$, where $C$ represents the circumference and $d$ represents the diameter. The diameter of the pothole is 18 inches (9 × 2). Substituting a diameter of 18 inches and 3.14 for the value of pi gives the following: $C = 3.14(18)$, or 56.52. Thus, the distance around the pothole is equal to 56.52 inches.

**31. B:** The area of a trapezoid can be found by using the formula $A = \frac{1}{2}(b_1 + b_2)h$, where $b_1$ and $b_2$ represent the lengths of the bases and $h$ represents the height of the trapezoid. Substituting the given base lengths and height reveals the following: $A = \frac{1}{2}(7 + 10)5$, which equals 42.5. Thus, the area of the trapezoid is 42.5 $cm^2$.

**32. D:** The sample space of rolling each die is 6. Thus, the sample space of rolling two dice is equal to the product of the sample spaces. 6 × 6 = 36; therefore, the sample space is equal to 36.

**33. C:** Flipping a coin one time has a sample space equal to 2, i.e., T or H. Flipping a coin 2 times has a sample space equal to 4, i.e., TT, HH, TH, HT. Flipping a coin 3 times has a sample space of 8, i.e., TTT, HHH, THT, HTH, TTH, HHT, THH, HTT. Notice that 2 is equal to $2^1$, 4 is equal to $2^2$, and 8 is equal to $2^3$. The sample space of flipping a coin 9 times is equal to $2^9$, or 512.

**34. B:** The events are independent since the spin of a spinner does not have an effect on the outcome of the flip of a coin. The probability of two independent events can be found using the formula $P(A\ and\ B) = P(A) \cdot P(B)$. The probability of landing on a number less than 5 is $\frac{4}{8}$ since there are 4 possible numbers less than 5 (1, 2, 3, and 4). The probability of getting tails is $\frac{1}{2}$. The probability of landing on a number less than 5 and getting tails is $\frac{4}{8} \cdot \frac{1}{2}$, which equals $\frac{4}{16}$, or $\frac{1}{4}$.

**35. D:** The events are independent since Ann replaces the first marble drawn. The probability of two independent events can be found using the formula $P(A\ and\ B) = P(A) \cdot P(B)$. The probability of pulling out a yellow marble is $\frac{8}{18}$. The probability of pulling out a green marble after the yellow marble has been replaced is $\frac{1}{18}$. The probability that Ann pulls out a yellow marble and then a green marble is $\frac{8}{18} \cdot \frac{1}{18}$, which equals $\frac{8}{324}$, which reduces to $\frac{2}{81}$.

**36. B:** The line graph shows the largest number of flights made during a month as 79 with the smallest number of flights made during a month as 54. The range is equal to the difference between the largest number of flights and smallest number of flights, i.e., 79 – 54 = 25. Therefore, the range is equal to 25.

**37. A:** The percentages of each type of tree are as follows: Apple tree – 20%; Peach tree – 44%; Fig tree – 29%, and Pear tree – 7%. The circle graph for Choice A accurately represents these percentages.

**38. A:** The median can be determined using any of the given graphical representations. However, a box-and-whiskers plot actually includes a line drawn for the median, thus clearly indicating the value of the median.

**39.** The correct answer is **304.** The median number of minutes can be determined by listing the number of minutes in order from least to greatest and calculating the average of the two middle values. The number of minutes can be written in ascending order as 255, 289, 291, 302, 306, 322, 411, and 418. The two middle values are 302 and 306. The average of these values can be determined by writing $\frac{302+306}{2}$, which equals 304. Thus, the median number of minutes is 304.

**40. B:** The average number (or mean) of incoming freshmen can be calculated by summing the numbers of incoming freshmen and dividing by the total number of years (or 10). Thus, the mean can be calculated by evaluating $\frac{76,146}{10}$, which equals 7,614.6. Since a fraction of a person cannot occur, the mean can be rounded to 7,615 freshmen.

# How to Overcome Test Anxiety

Just the thought of taking a test is enough to make most people a little nervous. A test is an important event that can have a long-term impact on your future, so it's important to take it seriously and it's natural to feel anxious about performing well. But just because anxiety is normal, that doesn't mean that it's helpful in test taking, or that you should simply accept it as part of your life. Anxiety can have a variety of effects. These effects can be mild, like making you feel slightly nervous, or severe, like blocking your ability to focus or remember even a simple detail.

If you experience test anxiety—whether severe or mild—it's important to know how to beat it. To discover this, first you need to understand what causes test anxiety.

## Causes of Test Anxiety

While we often think of anxiety as an uncontrollable emotional state, it can actually be caused by simple, practical things. One of the most common causes of test anxiety is that a person does not feel adequately prepared for their test. This feeling can be the result of many different issues such as poor study habits or lack of organization, but the most common culprit is time management. Starting to study too late, failing to organize your study time to cover all of the material, or being distracted while you study will mean that you're not well prepared for the test. This may lead to cramming the night before, which will cause you to be physically and mentally exhausted for the test. Poor time management also contributes to feelings of stress, fear, and hopelessness as you realize you are not well prepared but don't know what to do about it.

Other times, test anxiety is not related to your preparation for the test but comes from unresolved fear. This may be a past failure on a test, or poor performance on tests in general. It may come from comparing yourself to others who seem to be performing better or from the stress of living up to expectations. Anxiety may be driven by fears of the future—how failure on this test would affect your educational and career goals. These fears are often completely irrational, but they can still negatively impact your test performance.

## Elements of Test Anxiety

As mentioned earlier, test anxiety is considered to be an emotional state, but it has physical and mental components as well. Sometimes you may not even realize that you are suffering from test anxiety until you notice the physical symptoms. These can include trembling hands, rapid heartbeat, sweating, nausea, and tense muscles. Extreme anxiety may lead to fainting or vomiting. Obviously, any of these symptoms can have a negative impact on testing. It is important to recognize them as soon as they begin to occur so that you can address the problem before it damages your performance.

The mental components of test anxiety include trouble focusing and inability to remember learned information. During a test, your mind is on high alert, which can help you recall information and stay focused for an extended period of time. However, anxiety interferes with your mind's natural processes, causing you to blank out, even on the questions you know well. The strain of testing during anxiety makes it difficult to stay focused, especially on a test that may take several hours. Extreme anxiety can take a huge mental toll, making it difficult not only to recall test information but even to understand the test questions or pull your thoughts together.

## Effects of Test Anxiety

Test anxiety is like a disease—if left untreated, it will get progressively worse. Anxiety leads to poor performance, and this reinforces the feelings of fear and failure, which in turn lead to poor performances on subsequent tests. It can grow from a mild nervousness to a crippling condition. If allowed to progress, test anxiety can have a big impact on your schooling, and consequently on your future.

Test anxiety can spread to other parts of your life. Anxiety on tests can become anxiety in any stressful situation, and blanking on a test can turn into panicking in a job situation. But fortunately, you don't have to let anxiety rule your testing and determine your grades. There are a number of relatively simple steps you can take to move past anxiety and function normally on a test and in the rest of life.

## Physical Steps for Beating Test Anxiety

While test anxiety is a serious problem, the good news is that it can be overcome. It doesn't have to control your ability to think and remember information. While it may take time, you can begin taking steps today to beat anxiety.

Just as your first hint that you may be struggling with anxiety comes from the physical symptoms, the first step to treating it is also physical. Rest is crucial for having a clear, strong mind. If you are tired, it is much easier to give in to anxiety. But if you establish good sleep habits, your body and mind will be ready to perform optimally, without the strain of exhaustion. Additionally, sleeping well helps you to retain information better, so you're more likely to recall the answers when you see the test questions.

Getting good sleep means more than going to bed on time. It's important to allow your brain time to relax. Take study breaks from time to time so it doesn't get overworked, and don't study right before bed. Take time to rest your mind before trying to rest your body, or you may find it difficult to fall asleep.

Along with sleep, other aspects of physical health are important in preparing for a test. Good nutrition is vital for good brain function. Sugary foods and drinks may give a burst of energy but this burst is followed by a crash, both physically and emotionally. Instead, fuel your body with protein and vitamin-rich foods.

Also, drink plenty of water. Dehydration can lead to headaches and exhaustion, especially if your brain is already under stress from the rigors of the test. Particularly if your test is a long one, drink water during the breaks. And if possible, take an energy-boosting snack to eat between sections.

Along with sleep and diet, a third important part of physical health is exercise. Maintaining a steady workout schedule is helpful, but even taking 5-minute study breaks to walk can help get your blood pumping faster and clear your head. Exercise also releases endorphins, which contribute to a positive feeling and can help combat test anxiety.

When you nurture your physical health, you are also contributing to your mental health. If your body is healthy, your mind is much more likely to be healthy as well. So take time to rest, nourish your body with healthy food and water, and get moving as much as possible. Taking these physical steps will make you stronger and more able to take the mental steps necessary to overcome test anxiety.

## Mental Steps for Beating Test Anxiety

Working on the mental side of test anxiety can be more challenging, but as with the physical side, there are clear steps you can take to overcome it. As mentioned earlier, test anxiety often stems from lack of preparation, so the obvious solution is to prepare for the test. Effective studying may be the most important weapon you have for beating test anxiety, but you can and should employ several other mental tools to combat fear.

First, boost your confidence by reminding yourself of past success—tests or projects that you aced. If you're putting as much effort into preparing for this test as you did for those, there's no reason you should expect to fail here. Work hard to prepare; then trust your preparation.

Second, surround yourself with encouraging people. It can be helpful to find a study group, but be sure that the people you're around will encourage a positive attitude. If you spend time with others who are anxious or cynical, this will only contribute to your own anxiety. Look for others who are motivated to study hard from a desire to succeed, not from a fear of failure.

Third, reward yourself. A test is physically and mentally tiring, even without anxiety, and it can be helpful to have something to look forward to. Plan an activity following the test, regardless of the outcome, such as going to a movie or getting ice cream.

When you are taking the test, if you find yourself beginning to feel anxious, remind yourself that you know the material. Visualize successfully completing the test. Then take a few deep, relaxing breaths and return to it. Work through the questions carefully but with confidence, knowing that you are capable of succeeding.

Developing a healthy mental approach to test taking will also aid in other areas of life. Test anxiety affects more than just the actual test—it can be damaging to your mental health and even contribute to depression. It's important to beat test anxiety before it becomes a problem for more than testing.

## Study Strategy

Being prepared for the test is necessary to combat anxiety, but what does being prepared look like? You may study for hours on end and still not feel prepared. What you need is a strategy for test prep. The next few pages outline our recommended steps to help you plan out and conquer the challenge of preparation.

### Step 1: Scope Out the Test

Learn everything you can about the format (multiple choice, essay, etc.) and what will be on the test. Gather any study materials, course outlines, or sample exams that may be available. Not only will this help you to prepare, but knowing what to expect can help to alleviate test anxiety.

### Step 2: Map Out the Material

Look through the textbook or study guide and make note of how many chapters or sections it has. Then divide these over the time you have. For example, if a book has 15 chapters and you have five days to study, you need to cover three chapters each day. Even better, if you have the time, leave an extra day at the end for overall review after you have gone through the material in depth.

If time is limited, you may need to prioritize the material. Look through it and make note of which sections you think you already have a good grasp on, and which need review. While you are studying, skim quickly through the familiar sections and take more time on the challenging parts.

Write out your plan so you don't get lost as you go. Having a written plan also helps you feel more in control of the study, so anxiety is less likely to arise from feeling overwhelmed at the amount to cover.

### Step 3: Gather Your Tools

Decide what study method works best for you. Do you prefer to highlight in the book as you study and then go back over the highlighted portions? Or do you type out notes of the important information? Or is it helpful to make flashcards that you can carry with you? Assemble the pens, index cards, highlighters, post-it notes, and any other materials you may need so you won't be distracted by getting up to find things while you study.

If you're having a hard time retaining the information or organizing your notes, experiment with different methods. For example, try color-coding by subject with colored pens, highlighters, or post-it notes. If you learn better by hearing, try recording yourself reading your notes so you can listen while in the car, working out, or simply sitting at your desk. Ask a friend to quiz you from your flashcards, or try teaching someone the material to solidify it in your mind.

### Step 4: Create Your Environment

It's important to avoid distractions while you study. This includes both the obvious distractions like visitors and the subtle distractions like an uncomfortable chair (or a too-comfortable couch that makes you want to fall asleep). Set up the best study environment possible: good lighting and a comfortable work area. If background music helps you focus, you may want to turn it on, but otherwise keep the room quiet. If you are using a computer to take notes, be sure you don't have any other windows open, especially applications like social media, games, or anything else that could distract you. Silence your phone and turn off notifications. Be sure to keep water close by so you stay hydrated while you study (but avoid unhealthy drinks and snacks).

Also, take into account the best time of day to study. Are you freshest first thing in the morning? Try to set aside some time then to work through the material. Is your mind clearer in the afternoon or evening? Schedule your study session then. Another method is to study at the same time of day that you will take the test, so that your brain gets used to working on the material at that time and will be ready to focus at test time.

### Step 5: Study!

Once you have done all the study preparation, it's time to settle into the actual studying. Sit down, take a few moments to settle your mind so you can focus, and begin to follow your study plan. Don't give in to distractions or let yourself procrastinate. This is your time to prepare so you'll be ready to fearlessly approach the test. Make the most of the time and stay focused.

Of course, you don't want to burn out. If you study too long you may find that you're not retaining the information very well. Take regular study breaks. For example, taking five minutes out of every hour to walk briskly, breathing deeply and swinging your arms, can help your mind stay fresh.

As you get to the end of each chapter or section, it's a good idea to do a quick review. Remind yourself of what you learned and work on any difficult parts. When you feel that you've mastered the material, move on to the next part. At the end of your study session, briefly skim through your notes again.

But while review is helpful, cramming last minute is NOT. If at all possible, work ahead so that you won't need to fit all your study into the last day. Cramming overloads your brain with more information than it can process and retain, and your tired mind may struggle to recall even previously learned information when it is overwhelmed with last-minute study. Also, the urgent nature of cramming and the stress placed on your brain contribute to anxiety. You'll be more likely to go to the test feeling unprepared and having trouble thinking clearly.

So don't cram, and don't stay up late before the test, even just to review your notes at a leisurely pace. Your brain needs rest more than it needs to go over the information again. In fact, plan to finish your studies by noon or early afternoon the day before the test. Give your brain the rest of the day to relax or focus on other things, and get a good night's sleep. Then you will be fresh for the test and better able to recall what you've studied.

### Step 6: Take a Practice Test

Many courses offer sample tests, either online or in the study materials. This is an excellent resource to check whether you have mastered the material, as well as to prepare for the test format and environment.

Check the test format ahead of time: the number of questions, the type (multiple choice, free response, etc.), and the time limit. Then create a plan for working through them. For example, if you have 30 minutes to take a 60-question test, your limit is 30 seconds per question. Spend less time on the questions you know well so that you can take more time on the difficult ones.

If you have time to take several practice tests, take the first one open book, with no time limit. Work through the questions at your own pace and make sure you fully understand them. Gradually work up to taking a test under test conditions: sit at a desk with all study materials put away and set a timer. Pace yourself to make sure you finish the test with time to spare and go back to check your answers if you have time.

After each test, check your answers. On the questions you missed, be sure you understand why you missed them. Did you misread the question (tests can use tricky wording)? Did you forget the information? Or was it something you hadn't learned? Go back and study any shaky areas that the practice tests reveal.

Taking these tests not only helps with your grade, but also aids in combating test anxiety. If you're already used to the test conditions, you're less likely to worry about it, and working through tests until you're scoring well gives you a confidence boost. Go through the practice tests until you feel comfortable, and then you can go into the test knowing that you're ready for it.

## Test Tips

On test day, you should be confident, knowing that you've prepared well and are ready to answer the questions. But aside from preparation, there are several test day strategies you can employ to maximize your performance.

First, as stated before, get a good night's sleep the night before the test (and for several nights before that, if possible). Go into the test with a fresh, alert mind rather than staying up late to study.

Try not to change too much about your normal routine on the day of the test. It's important to eat a nutritious breakfast, but if you normally don't eat breakfast at all, consider eating just a protein bar. If you're a coffee drinker, go ahead and have your normal coffee. Just make sure you time it so that the caffeine doesn't wear off right in the middle of your test. Avoid sugary beverages, and drink enough water to stay hydrated but not so much that you need a restroom break 10 minutes into the test. If your test isn't first thing in the morning, consider going for a walk or doing a light workout before the test to get your blood flowing.

Allow yourself enough time to get ready, and leave for the test with plenty of time to spare so you won't have the anxiety of scrambling to arrive in time. Another reason to be early is to select a good seat. It's helpful to sit away from doors and windows, which can be distracting. Find a good seat, get out your supplies, and settle your mind before the test begins.

When the test begins, start by going over the instructions carefully, even if you already know what to expect. Make sure you avoid any careless mistakes by following the directions.

Then begin working through the questions, pacing yourself as you've practiced. If you're not sure on an answer, don't spend too much time on it, and don't let it shake your confidence. Either skip it and come back later, or eliminate as many wrong answers as possible and guess among the remaining ones. Don't dwell on these questions as you continue—put them out of your mind and focus on what lies ahead.

Be sure to read all of the answer choices, even if you're sure the first one is the right answer. Sometimes you'll find a better one if you keep reading. But don't second-guess yourself if you do immediately know the answer. Your gut instinct is usually right. Don't let test anxiety rob you of the information you know.

If you have time at the end of the test (and if the test format allows), go back and review your answers. Be cautious about changing any, since your first instinct tends to be correct, but make sure you didn't misread any of the questions or accidentally mark the wrong answer choice. Look over any you skipped and make an educated guess.

At the end, leave the test feeling confident. You've done your best, so don't waste time worrying about your performance or wishing you could change anything. Instead, celebrate the successful completion of this test. And finally, use this test to learn how to deal with anxiety even better next time.

**Review Video: Test Anxiety**
Visit mometrix.com/academy and enter code: 100340

## Important Qualification

Not all anxiety is created equal. If your test anxiety is causing major issues in your life beyond the classroom or testing center, or if you are experiencing troubling physical symptoms related to your anxiety, it may be a sign of a serious physiological or psychological condition. If this sounds like your situation, we strongly encourage you to seek professional help.

# How to Overcome Your Fear of Math

Not again. You're sitting in math class, look down at your test, and immediately start to panic. Your stomach is in knots, your heart is racing, and you break out in a cold sweat. You're staring at the paper, but everything looks like it's written in a foreign language. Even though you studied, you're blanking out on how to begin solving these problems.

Does this sound familiar? If so, then you're not alone! You may be like millions of other people who experience math anxiety. Anxiety about performing well in math is a common experience for students of all ages. In this article, we'll discuss what math anxiety is, common misconceptions about learning math, and tips and strategies for overcoming math anxiety.

## What Is Math Anxiety?

Psychologist Mark H. Ashcraft explains math anxiety as a feeling of tension, apprehension, or fear that interferes with math performance. Having math anxiety negatively impacts people's beliefs about themselves and what they can achieve. It hinders achievement within the math classroom and affects the successful application of mathematics in the real world.

### Symptoms and Signs of Math Anxiety

To overcome math anxiety, you must recognize its symptoms. Becoming aware of the signs of math anxiety is the first step in addressing and resolving these fears.

#### *Negative Self-Talk*

If you have math anxiety, you've most likely said at least one of these statements to yourself:

- "I hate math."
- "I'm not good at math."
- "I'm not a math person."

The way we speak to ourselves and think about ourselves matters. Our thoughts become our words, our words become our actions, and our actions become our habits. Thinking negatively about math creates a self-fulfilling prophecy. In other words, if you take an idea as a fact, then it will come true because your behaviors will align to match it.

#### *Avoidance*

Some people who are fearful or anxious about math will tend to avoid it altogether. Avoidance can manifest in the following ways:

- Lack of engagement with math content
- Not completing homework and other assignments
- Not asking for help when needed
- Skipping class
- Avoiding math-related courses and activities

Avoidance is one of the most harmful impacts of math anxiety. If you steer clear of math at all costs, then you can't set yourself up for the success you deserve.

### Lack of Motivation

Students with math anxiety may experience a lack of motivation. They may struggle to find the incentive to get engaged with what they view as a frightening subject. These students are often overwhelmed, making it difficult for them to complete or even start math assignments.

### Procrastination

Another symptom of math anxiety is procrastination. Students may voluntarily delay or postpone their classwork and assignments, even if they know there will be a negative consequence for doing so. Additionally, they may choose to wait until the last minute to start projects and homework, even when they know they need more time to put forth their best effort.

### Physiological Reactions

Many people with a fear of math experience physiological side effects. These may include an increase in heart rate, sweatiness, shakiness, nausea, and irregular breathing. These symptoms make it difficult to focus on the math content, causing the student even more stress and fear.

### Strong Emotional Responses

Math anxiety also affects people on an emotional level. Responding to math content with strong emotions such as panic, anger, or despair can be a sign of math anxiety.

### Low Test Scores and Performance

Low achievement can be both a symptom and a cause of math anxiety. When someone does not take the steps needed to perform well on tests and assessments, they are less likely to pass. The more they perform poorly, the more they accept this poor performance as a fact that can't be changed.

### Feeling Alone

People who experience math anxiety feel like they are the only ones struggling, even if the math they are working on is challenging to many people. Feeling isolated in what they perceive as failure can trigger tension or nervousness.

### Feeling of Permanency

Math anxiety can feel very permanent. You may assume that you are naturally bad at math and always will be. Viewing math as a natural ability rather than a skill that can be learned causes people to believe that nothing will help them improve. They take their current math abilities as fact and assume that they can't be changed. As a result, they give up, stop trying to improve, and avoid engaging with math altogether.

### Lack of Confidence

People with low self-confidence in math tend to feel awkward and incompetent when asked to solve a math problem. They don't feel comfortable taking chances or risks when problem-solving because they second-guess themselves and assume they are incorrect. They don't trust in their ability to learn the content and solve problems correctly.

### Panic

A general sense of unexplained panic is also a sign of math anxiety. You may feel a sudden sense of fear that triggers physical reactions, even when there is no apparent reason for such a response.

## Causes Of Math Anxiety

Math anxiety can start at a young age and may have one or more underlying causes. Common causes of math anxiety include the following:

### *The Attitude of Parents or Guardians*

Parents often put pressure on their children to perform well in school. Although their intentions are usually good, this pressure can lead to anxiety, especially if the student is struggling with a subject or class.

Perhaps your parents or others in your life hold negative predispositions about math based on their own experiences. For instance, if your mother once claimed she was not good at math, then you might have incorrectly interpreted this as a predisposed trait that was passed down to you.

### *Teacher Influence*

Students often pick up on their teachers' attitudes about the content being taught. If a teacher is happy and excited about math, students are more likely to mirror these emotions. However, if a teacher lacks enthusiasm or genuine interest, then students are more inclined to disengage.

Teachers have a responsibility to cultivate a welcoming classroom culture that is accepting of mistakes. When teachers blame students for not understanding a concept, they create a hostile classroom environment where mistakes are not tolerated. This tension increases student stress and anxiety, creating conditions that are not conducive to inquiry and learning. Instead, when teachers normalize mistakes as a natural part of the problem-solving process, they give their students the freedom to explore and grapple with the math content. In such an environment, students feel comfortable taking chances because they are not afraid of being wrong.

Students need teachers that can help when they're having problems understanding difficult concepts. In doing so, educators may need to change how they teach the content. Since different people have unique learning styles, it's the job of the teacher to adapt to the needs of each student. Additionally, teachers should encourage students to explore alternate problem-solving strategies, even if it's not the preferred method of the educator.

### *Fear of Being Wrong*

Embarrassing situations can be traumatic, especially for young children and adolescents. These experiences can stay with people through their adult lives. Those with math anxiety may experience a fear of being wrong, especially in front of a group of peers. This fear can be paralyzing, interfering with the student's concentration and ability to focus on the problem at hand.

### *Timed Assessments*

Timed assessments can help improve math fluency, but they often create unnecessary pressure for students to complete an unrealistic number of problems within a specified timeframe. Many studies have shown that timed assessments often result in increased levels of anxiety, reducing a student's overall competence and ability to problem-solve.

# Debunking Math Myths

There are lots of myths about math that are related to the causes and development of math-related anxiety. Although these myths have been proven to be false, many people take them as fact. Let's go over a few of the most common myths about learning math.

## Myth: Men Are Better at Math Than Women

Math has a reputation for being a male-dominant subject, but this doesn't mean that men are inherently better at math than women. Many famous mathematical discoveries have been made by women. Katherine Johnson, Dame Mary Lucy Cartwright, and Marjorie Lee Brown are just a few of the many famous women mathematicians. Expecting to be good or bad at math because of your gender sets you up for stress and confusion. Math is a skill that can be learned, just like cooking or riding a bike.

## Myth: There Is Only One Good Way to Solve Math Problems

There are many ways to get the correct answer when it comes to math. No two people have the same brain, so everyone takes a slightly different approach to problem-solving. Moreover, there isn't one way of problem-solving that's superior to another. Your way of working through a problem might differ from someone else's, and that is okay. Math can be a highly individualized process, so the best method for you should be the one that makes you feel the most comfortable and makes the most sense to you.

## Myth: Math Requires a Good Memory

For many years, mathematics was taught through memorization. However, learning in such a way hinders the development of critical thinking and conceptual understanding. These skill sets are much more valuable than basic memorization. For instance, you might be great at memorizing mathematical formulas, but if you don't understand what they mean, then you can't apply them to different scenarios in the real world. When a student is working from memory, they are limited in the strategies available to them to problem-solve. In other words, they assume there is only one correct way to do the math, which is the method they memorized. Having a variety of problem-solving options can help students figure out which method works best for them. Additionally, it provides students with a better understanding of how and why certain mathematical strategies work. While memorization can be helpful in some instances, it is not an absolute requirement for mathematicians.

## Myth: Math Is Not Creative

Math requires imagination and intuition. Contrary to popular belief, it is a highly creative field. Mathematical creativity can help in developing new ways to think about and solve problems. Many people incorrectly assume that all things are either creative or analytical. However, this black-and-white view is limiting because the field of mathematics involves both creativity and logic.

## Myth: Math Isn't Supposed To Be Fun

Whoever told you that math isn't supposed to be fun is a liar. There are tons of math-based activities and games that foster friendly competition and engagement. Math is often best learned through play, and lots of mobile apps and computer games exemplify this.

Additionally, math can be an exceptionally collaborative and social experience. Studying or working through problems with a friend often makes the process a lot more fun. The excitement and satisfaction of solving a difficult problem with others is quite rewarding. Math can be fun if you look for ways to make it more collaborative and enjoyable.

### Myth: Not Everyone Is Capable of Learning Math

There's no such thing as a "math person." Although many people think that you're either good at math or you're not, this is simply not true. Everyone is capable of learning and applying mathematics. However, not everyone learns the same way. Since each person has a different learning style, the trick is to find the strategies and learning tools that work best for you. Some people learn best through hands-on experiences, and others find success through the use of visual aids. Others are auditory learners and learn best by hearing and listening. When people are overwhelmed or feel that math is too hard, it's often because they haven't found the learning strategy that works best for them.

### Myth: Good Mathematicians Work Quickly and Never Make Mistakes

There is no prize for finishing first in math. It's not a race, and speed isn't a measure of your ability. Good mathematicians take their time to ensure their work is accurate. As you gain more experience and practice, you will naturally become faster and more confident.

Additionally, everyone makes mistakes, including good mathematicians. Mistakes are a normal part of the problem-solving process, and they're not a bad thing. The important thing is that we take the time to learn from our mistakes, understand where our misconceptions are, and move forward.

### Myth: You Don't Need Math in the Real World

Our day-to-day lives are so infused with mathematical concepts that we often don't even realize when we're using math in the real world. In fact, most people tend to underestimate how much we do math in our everyday lives. It's involved in an enormous variety of daily activities such as shopping, baking, finances, and gardening, as well as in many careers, including architecture, nursing, design, and sales.

## Tips and Strategies for Overcoming Math Anxiety

If your anxiety is getting in the way of your level of mathematical engagement, then there are lots of steps you can take. Check out the strategies below to start building confidence in math today.

### Focus on Understanding, Not Memorization

Don't drive yourself crazy trying to memorize every single formula or mathematical process. Instead, shift your attention to understanding concepts. Those who prioritize memorization over conceptual understanding tend to have lower achievement levels in math. Students who memorize may be able to complete some math, but they don't understand the process well enough to apply it to different situations. Memorization comes with time and practice, but it won't help alleviate math anxiety. On the other hand, conceptual understanding will give you the building blocks of knowledge you need to build up your confidence.

## Replace Negative Self-Talk with Positive Self-Talk

Start to notice how you think about yourself. Whenever you catch yourself thinking something negative, try replacing that thought with a positive affirmation. Instead of continuing the negative thought, pause to reframe the situation. For ideas on how to get started, take a look at the table below:

| Instead of thinking... | Try thinking... |
|---|---|
| "I can't do this math."<br>"I'm not a math person." | "I'm up for the challenge, and I'm training my brain in math." |
| "This problem is too hard." | "This problem is hard, so this might take some time and effort. I know I can do this." |
| "I give up." | "What strategies can help me solve this problem?" |
| "I made a mistake, so I'm not good at this." | "Everyone makes mistakes. Mistakes help me to grow and understand." |
| "I'll never be smart enough." | "I can figure this out, and I am smart enough." |

## Practice Mindfulness

Practicing mindfulness and focusing on your breathing can help alleviate some of the physical symptoms of math anxiety. By taking deep breaths, you can remind your nervous system that you are not in immediate danger. Doing so will reduce your heart rate and help with any irregular breathing or shakiness. Taking the edge off of the physiological effects of anxiety will clear your mind, allowing your brain to focus its energy on problem-solving.

## Do Some Math Every Day

Think about learning math as if you were learning a foreign language. If you don't use it, you lose it. If you don't practice your math skills regularly, you'll have a harder time achieving comprehension and fluency. Set some amount of time aside each day, even if it's just for a few minutes, to practice. It might take some discipline to build a habit around this, but doing so will help increase your mathematical self-assurance.

## Use All of Your Resources

Everyone has a different learning style, and there are plenty of resources out there to support all learners. When you get stuck on a math problem, think about the tools you have access to, and use them when applicable. Such resources may include flashcards, graphic organizers, study guides, interactive notebooks, and peer study groups. All of these are great tools to accommodate your individual learning style. Finding the tools and resources that work for your learning style will give you the confidence you need to succeed.

## Realize That You Aren't Alone

Remind yourself that lots of other people struggle with math anxiety, including teachers, nurses, and even successful mathematicians. You aren't the only one who panics when faced with a new or challenging problem. It's probably much more common than you think. Realizing that you aren't alone in your experience can help put some distance between yourself and the emotions you feel about math. It also helps to normalize the anxiety and shift your perspective.

### Ask Questions

If there's a concept you don't understand and you've tried everything you can, then it's okay to ask for help! You can always ask your teacher or professor for help. If you're not learning math in a traditional classroom, you may want to join a study group, work with a tutor, or talk to your friends. More often than not, you aren't the only one of your peers who needs clarity on a mathematical concept. Seeking understanding is a great way to increase self-confidence in math.

### Remember That There's More Than One Way To Solve A Problem

Since everyone learns differently, it's best to focus on understanding a math problem with an approach that makes sense to you. If the way it's being taught is confusing to you, don't give up. Instead, work to understand the problem using a different technique. There's almost always more than one problem-solving method when it comes to math. Don't get stressed if one of them doesn't make sense to you. Instead, shift your focus to what does make sense. Chances are high that you know more than you think you do.

### Visualization

Visualization is the process of creating images in your mind's eye. Picture yourself as a successful, confident mathematician. Think about how you would feel and how you would behave. What would your work area look like? How would you organize your belongings? The more you focus on something, the more likely you are to achieve it. Visualizing teaches your brain that you can achieve whatever it is that you want. Thinking about success in mathematics will lead to acting like a successful mathematician. This, in turn, leads to actual success.

### Focus on the Easiest Problems First

To increase your confidence when working on a math test or assignment, try solving the easiest problems first. Doing so will remind you that you are successful in math and that you do have what it takes. This process will increase your belief in yourself, giving you the confidence you need to tackle more complex problems.

### Find a Support Group

A study buddy, tutor, or peer group can go a long way in decreasing math-related anxiety. Such support systems offer lots of benefits, including a safe place to ask questions, additional practice with mathematical concepts, and an understanding of other problem-solving explanations that may work better for you. Equipping yourself with a support group is one of the fastest ways to eliminate math anxiety.

### Reward Yourself for Working Hard

Recognize the amount of effort you're putting in to overcome your math anxiety. It's not an easy task, so you deserve acknowledgement. Surround yourself with people who will provide you with the positive reinforcement you deserve.

## Remember, You Can Do This!

Conquering a fear of math can be challenging, but there are lots of strategies that can help you out. Your own beliefs about your mathematical capabilities can limit your potential. Working toward a growth mindset can have a tremendous impact on decreasing math-related anxiety and building confidence. By knowing the symptoms of math anxiety and recognizing common misconceptions about learning math, you can develop a plan to address your fear of math. Utilizing the strategies discussed can help you overcome this anxiety and build the confidence you need to succeed.

# Thank You

We at Mometrix would like to extend our heartfelt thanks to you, our friend and patron, for allowing us to play a part in your journey. It is a privilege to serve people from all walks of life who are unified in their commitment to building the best future they can for themselves.

The preparation you devote to these important testing milestones may be the most valuable educational opportunity you have for making a real difference in your life. We encourage you to put your heart into it—that feeling of succeeding, overcoming, and yes, conquering will be well worth the hours you've invested.

We want to hear your story, your struggles and your successes, and if you see any opportunities for us to improve our materials so we can help others even more effectively in the future, please share that with us as well. **The team at Mometrix would be absolutely thrilled to hear from you!** So please, send us an email (support@mometrix.com) and let's stay in touch.

If you'd like some additional help, check out these other resources we offer for your exam:

http://MometrixFlashcards.com/MCA

# Online Resources

Due to our efforts to try to keep this book to a manageable length, we've created a link that will give you access to all of your online resources:

**mometrix.com/resources719/ssmcag7math**

# It's Your Moment, Let's Celebrate It!

**Share your story @mometrixtestpreparation**